The
Heart-Mind
Connection

The
Heart-Mind
Connection

How Emotions Contribute to Heart Disease and What to Do About It

Windsor Ting, M.D., and
Gregory Fricchione, M.D.

McGraw·Hill

New York   Chicago   San Francisco   Lisbon   London   Madrid   Mexico City
Milan   New Delhi   San Juan   Seoul   Singapore   Sydney   Toronto

Library of Congress Cataloging-in-Publication Data

Ting, Windsor.
    The heart-mind connection : how emotions contribute to heart disease and what
to do about it / Windsor Ting and Gregory Fricchione.
        p.   cm.
    Includes bibliographical references.
    ISBN 0-07-139026-X
    1. Heart—Diseases—Psychological aspects.   I. Fricchione, Gregory.   II. Title.

RC682.T57   2006
616.1'2—dc22   2005013718

Illustrations on pp. 10, 21, and 116 copyright © by John Nebesney

1 2 3 4 5 6 7 8 9 0 DOC/DOC 0 9 8 7 6 5

ISBN 0-07-139026-X

Interior design by Rattray Design

McGraw-Hill books are available at special quantity discounts to use as premiums and
sales promotions, or for use in corporate training programs. For more information, please
write to the Director of Special Sales, Professional Publishing, McGraw-Hill, Two Penn
Plaza, New York, NY 10121-2298. Or contact your local bookstore.

The patient names and identifying information contained in this book have been changed
to protect their privacy.

This book is printed on acid-free paper.

To our wives, Mary Lou and Kathryn, and our children—Peter, Marion, and Olivia and Kristen, Marielle, and Jon—with all of whom we are blessed to travel the road.

Contents

Foreword

IN THE MORE THAN thirty years I have been working on mental health issues, I have seen dramatic changes in the understanding and treatment of depressive illness. Those who have suffered with depression have always known how devastating it can be. Sir Winston Churchill referred to his illness as a "black dog" he needed to tame. We have now found that depression takes a tremendous toll not only on the affected individual but also on families, workplaces, communities, and indeed even on countries.

Some years ago, in the Medical Outcomes Study done by Rand Corporation, depression was found to be the second-most disabling illness in the United States. With the development by C. J. Murray and A. D. Lopez of a measure called "Disability Adjusted Life Years (DALYs)," which enables us to quantify the "burden of disease," we have recently learned how pervasive and destructive depressive illness is. By the year 2020, the World Health Organization expects it to be the second-most disabling of all illnesses in the world.

Major depression can ruin lives and, if left untreated, can lead to suicide. Suicide is so prevalent across all age groups that the U.S. surgeon general has named it a major public health concern. Suicide and suicide attempts, which plague emergency rooms around the country, are a tragic demonstration of the burden of disease associated with depression.

There are also new data that come from research on the risk of cardiac disease. Depression—along with a bad cholesterol profile, cigarette smoking, and obesity—is now known to be an independent risk factor for heart disease. Moreover, for those who already have had a cardiac event such as a heart attack or myocardial infarction, the likelihood of recurrence and death from heart disease is significantly greater if they are depressed. In effect, there is an unholy alliance between cardiac disease, the number one illness burden, and depression, the number two illness burden.

My 1998 book, *Helping Someone with Mental Illness*, has a chapter on depression that emphasizes the fact that it can be diagnosed and treated more effectively than ever with new antidepressants and innovative psychotherapies such as cognitive behavioral therapy. Today new somatic therapies such as transcranial magnetic stimulation and vagal nerve stimulation are being tested to see whether they can be used as treatments. There is cause for hope.

It appears that the message is starting to filter through to Americans about depression's treatability. A recent report states that the percentage of Americans seeking a physician's treatment for the illness tripled in the decade ending in 1997. This is good news, but we still have a long way to go.

In an easy-to-understand, very accessible style, this excellent book, *The Heart-Mind Connection: How Emotions Contribute to Heart Disease and What to Do About It* by Dr. Windsor Ting and Dr. Greg Fricchione, brings to the reader the latest information about how to recognize depression and other negative emotions, how to deal with certain myths that have grown up around them, and how to seek and obtain the best-quality treatment. This is essential information for anyone at risk for heart problems and certainly for anyone stricken with cardiac disease, given what we now know about the mutually destructive effects of these two illnesses.

In this book, the reader will learn the signs of depression and other important conditions that affect your heart. You will gain a better understanding of negative emotions by learning about the chemical changes that occur in the brain during times of stress and depression.

You will be enlightened about psychosocial risk factors for cardiac illness. The antidepressive treatments will be reviewed, as will ways to combat stress and anger, and you will get tips about how to customize with your doctor the most successful regimen in order to help yourself. This is extremely important when one is dealing with depressive illness and/or cardiac disease.

In the past, the significance of heart disease for women was ignored; the research focused only on men. Fortunately, this oversight is now being corrected. Women suffer greatly from this illness, and because they are also more likely than men to be depressed, the messages delivered in this book will be particularly significant for them.

One of the most important antidotes to a depressive mood is optimism.

University of Pennsylvania professor of psychology Martin Seligman, Ph.D., once came to the Carter Center to talk about the differences between learned helplessness and learned optimism. This book encourages optimism by sharing the knowledge that depression is diagnosable and treatable and that the overwhelming majority of people who are affected can lead normal, happy, and productive lives. This can be true even for those who are living life with heart disease.

—Rosalynn Carter

Acknowledgments

We would like to acknowledge the enormous help of many individuals in creating this book. In particular, we thank George Ryan for his assistance in the research and manuscript preparation. Also, special thanks to Natasha Graf, our editor, for believing in the idea behind this book. We would like to acknowledge John Nebesney for the use of his illustrations. And finally, thanks to the late Michael Cohn, our literary agent.

Introduction

IN GENERAL, CARDIAC surgeons and psychiatrists take care of very different groups of patients. Although we hear a lot in the media about mind-body connections, in everyday practice, psychiatrists and surgeons don't work together very often.

In this book, we deliberately share our different perspectives to give you a more wide-angle view of heart disease. You'll read the point of view of a surgeon who uses a scalpel, sutures, and modern surgical equipment to help the heart work better and longer along with that of a psychiatrist who listens, communicates, diagnoses, and prescribes medications that can profoundly affect the brain and improve disordered mood, behavior, and thinking.

I, Dr. Ting, am a heart surgeon in private practice in New York City, and my coauthor, Dr. Fricchione, is a psychiatrist and the director of the Division of Psychiatry and Medicine at Massachusetts General Hospital in Boston, as well as a faculty member at Harvard Medical School.

In my practice as a heart specialist, I find that patients and their families are not aware of the important relationship between negative emotions and heart disease. Several years ago, I noticed that following open-heart surgery, many patients were depressed and anxious. It became clear that these emotions affected their recovery. With further research, it became obvious that a strong interrelationship exists between heart disease and different emotional states. Unfortunately, few people are aware of this association. I started incorporating what I learned in this area into my clinical practice. This book describes how I learned to help people with heart disease and those who require open-heart surgery handle this common problem.

In his role as a psychiatrist working on medical and surgical units, Dr. Fricchione observed patients whose heart disease had resulted in depression and other emotional disorders. He also knew that these same emotional states increase the risk for heart disease or worsen a preexisting heart condition. We decided to compare clinical experiences and found that our shared knowledge was enhanced by our different perspectives, and we wanted to relate what we learned in the hope that others will benefit.

Depression and Heart Disease: Ignoring an Important Connection

In my estimation, 20 to 25 percent of patients hospitalized with heart disease have major depression and another 20 percent have minor depression. In fact, depression is so frequent in people with coronary artery disease that those doctors who notice it at all don't regard it as anything special and assume it has little lasting effect. The truth is that doctors infrequently diagnose or treat depression in their heart patients. For their part, patients rarely acknowledge depression because of its social stigma (discussed further in Chapter 3). Many also don't want to bother their doctors. Even when patients do admit to being depressed, they often resist psychiatric help or treatment with antidepressants.

Given what medical researchers have discovered about the association between depression and cardiovascular disease, it is unfortunate that such a state of affairs still exists. Many doctors have heard about depression's links to cardiac problems but aren't familiar with the following four simple facts.

1. Depression has been correlated with the development of coronary artery disease among healthy people in several studies. We talk about this more in Chapter 4.
2. Among people who already have coronary artery disease, depression can precipitate a heart attack and/or lead to an earlier death.
3. After a heart attack, those who are depressed are three to four times more likely to die than those who are not.
4. Following cardiac surgery, a large percentage of patients develop depression severe enough to interfere with the surgical outcome and their physical recovery.

After taking care of many heart patients, I initially thought that the most depressed people were the ones at highest risk of a heart attack; that is, the more serious the depression, the greater the risk of coronary artery disease and related complications. While this is so, I now believe that even low levels of depression can lead to cardiac problems as well.

Depression After a Heart Attack

Major depression affects about one in five people after a heart attack (acute myocardial infarction) and is associated with an increased risk for further cardiac trouble and death. Depressed people recovering from a heart attack are two to seven times more likely to die than similar nondepressed people. This may be because, in general, depressed people don't exercise much and often have a lower blood level of good cholesterol (HDL) and a high level of triglycerides. Those who are depressed often have lower scores in tests for mental health, energy, general health, pain, overall function, well-being, and quality of life. Depressed patients are also more likely to smoke, suffer anxiety, and show hostility to other people.

After cardiac rehabilitation and exercise training, depression is usually lessened, as are anxiety, hostility, and preoccupation with physical symptoms. In addition, exercise capacity, percentage of body fat,

HDL and triglyceride levels, and quality of life also show improvements. You can read about this in more detail in Chapter 5.

Depression After Cardiac Surgery

Studies have shown that many patients are depressed before cardiac surgery and even more patients are discouraged during the first few weeks after cardiac surgery. During recovery after a coronary bypass operation, depression interferes with functional improvement, provides a poor quality of life, and is a potential risk factor for another heart attack. Depression is also linked to poor adherence to medication regimens, longer hospitalization, increased rates of readmission to hospital, sexual dysfunction, and an inability to work.

Cognitive problems, including memory loss and difficulty in concentrating, are very common after coronary bypass surgery. Even though cognitive problems are real complications after heart surgery, depression is also associated with cognitive impairment or makes an underlying impairment worse. This means that, with treatment of depression, certain cognitive difficulties may be reversed. We talk about this more in Chapter 6.

The Eight Heart-Mind Conspirators

Heart-mind conspirators are what we call emotions or perceptions that can be linked with damage to our cardiovascular system. We've identified eight heart-mind conspirators, discussed in more detail in Chapter 1.

1. Depression (see Chapters 3 through 6)
2. Anxiety (see Chapter 7)
3. Anger and hostility (see Chapter 8)
4. Social isolation (see Chapter 9)
5. Chronic life stresses like a difficult job or stressful relationships (see Chapter 10)

6. Acute life stresses like loss of job, divorce, death of a loved one, war, and so on (see Chapter 10)
7. Panic attacks (see Chapter 11)
8. Daily and seasonal rhythms (see Chapter 12)

Throughout these chapters, we look at our mind-body connections to see how these heart-mind conspirators physically undermine our health.

The Mind and Body Working Together

Chapters 13 and 14 provide you with several practical options to stay well if you are healthy and to get well if you are ill: survival strategies for heart patients and taking antidepressants, respectively. You'll find out how emotions actually cause cardiac trouble. Some of the things that happen are simple, such as increased blood turbulence inside an artery. Other concepts may at first seem strange—you may not have thought of your mind and body working together in these ways. In Chapter 15, you find the physical explanation of much of what we have shared in earlier chapters.

Women and Heart Disease

Coronary artery disease is the leading cause of death and disability for American women. Prior to menopause, estrogen and other factors protect women from coronary artery disease. After menopause, the protective effect of estrogen is diminished, and women gradually catch up to men in their risk of heart disease. In fact, a postmenopausal woman is ten times more likely to die of coronary artery disease than of breast cancer or hip fracture. One in eight women aged forty-five to fifty-four has signs of coronary heart disease. The same holds true for one in three women older than sixty-five. In addition, once women develop signs of coronary artery disease, they tend to do much worse compared to men. The hospital mortality rate for heart attack is 15 percent for women and 10 percent for men, and more women than men die within a year of having a heart attack.

Depression is more common in women; the reported incidence is two times higher than in men. The causes of depression are also different between the two genders: social isolation, quality of relationships, and change in an existing relationship are frequent causes in women.

Estrogen replacement therapy is on the minds of many women, but not necessarily as a way to protect their hearts. Chapters 16 through 18 discuss women's hearts in more detail, look at how emotions uniquely affect women's hearts, and examine the connection between women's hearts and minds and estrogen replacement therapy.

This book will enable you to recognize how your emotions may be affecting your heart. If you believe that your emotions may be harming your cardiovascular health, you should discuss the matter with your doctor before problems develop or worsen. It is also our hope that this book will empower you to communicate with your doctor in an understandable way. Being able to do so and finding effective help—for yourself or someone close to you—may be the single most important effort you can make to achieve a long, enjoyable life.

The
Heart-Mind
Connection

PART I

Uncovering the Heart-Mind Connection

1

Understanding the Heart-Mind Conspirators

Robert, a retired businessman in Portland, Maine, had coronary artery disease for many years. As a result, when he died from a massive heart attack, no one was surprised. Although Robert suffered from coronary artery disease, he still lived a full life. Could the heart attack have been prevented? Would a healthier diet and more exercise have been helpful? Even though these are proven measures of preventing heart disease, they may not have been helpful in Robert's case. But there may have been more to it. At the time of his death, Robert was living alone. He never remarried after a divorce many years earlier. Martha, his daughter and only child, had always been the major focus in his life. He was a proud father at her many graduations, provided encouragement in her numerous careers, and treasured her frequent weekend visits. Robert was devastated when Martha was diagnosed with breast cancer and died three years later. It was six months after his daughter's death that his housekeeper found him dead from a confirmed massive heart attack.

Was Robert's heart attack after his daughter's death a coincidence given his grief and loneliness? Or did the timing of the two events suggest a causal association? And, what exactly was the relationship if one existed? This book seeks to answer those questions.

PEOPLE USE THE TERM *heartbreak* to describe an overwhelming sadness or loss. The expression is eloquent: it says that the heart, a perfectly engineered blood pump, can be broken by a deep, powerful emotion. Most people have felt heartbreak on a firsthand basis. Not surprisingly, this metaphor can be found in literature, songs, and mythologies spanning more than two thousand years. The Bible, Shakespeare's plays, poetry of e. e. cummings, and songs of Elvis Presley are just a few examples. But is heartbreak just a metaphor?

The part of your brain that mediates cardiac pain is adjacent to an area important for human social attachment. That suggests how grief can bring on chest pain. But can a deep emotion really damage the heart? While people have realized a major illness like heart disease can bring on negative emotions, only recently have doctors realized that the reverse is also possible; that is, negative emotions can bring on heart disease or worsen an existing heart condition. What is this relationship between the mind and the heart?

Meet the Heart-Mind Conspirators

Heart-mind conspirators are what we call emotions or perceptions that can be linked with damage to our cardiovascular system. We discuss eight heart-mind conspirators, and while there are others, the evidence is most convincing regarding these eight.

1. *Depression.* This conspirator is the one linked to heart disease by the firmest evidence. It also has psychosocial implications, which means that when depression interacts with other stresses (such as the ones on this list), it builds up the total amount of psychosocial stress you are feeling, and more psychosocial stress increases your cardiac risk level. In addition, psychosocial stresses can interact with other kinds of stress and with other cardiac risk factors to increase your total cardiac risk. For example, depressed people who smoke have a higher cardiac risk than depressed people who don't smoke.

2. *Anxiety.* Acute anxiety disorders have been studied for some time, but only recently have medical studies been done on people who have never been psychiatrically treated for these conditions. High anx-

iety levels in these people are linked more to sudden cardiac death and less to heart attacks, suggesting that ventricular arrhythmias are the mechanism responsible for death.

3. *Anger and hostility (or type A behavior)*. This condition is characterized by competition and impatience, but the component of type A behavior that is most likely to contribute to heart disease is hostility. Hostility includes such character traits as anger, cynicism, and mistrust, all of which have strong ties to heart trouble. The higher the anger level, the greater the likelihood of a heart attack. In addition, hostile people are likely to smoke, drink too much, have a poor diet, and be obese.

4. *Social isolation*. Isolation can be thought of in both quantitative and qualitative ways. Family, friends, and group activities make up your social network. Thus, the more people you interact with on a daily basis, the smaller the chance there is of your becoming socially isolated. However, a person can have scores of acquaintances who provide little emotional support, while another person can have only two or three friends who contribute major emotional support. In general, people with a very small social network have two to three times the risk of coronary artery disease, and those with little or no emotional support have an even higher risk.

5. *Chronic and subacute life stress*. Chronic stress happens frequently over a long period of time. One of the most dangerous kinds of chronic stress is job strain—the tension that develops from high-demand work with little decision-making opportunity. Work situations that include job strain, low level of control, and high work demand with low reward are all known to increase the risk of coronary artery disease. Subacute life stress consists of the accumulation of stressful events over a period of months to years. These everyday hassles are too insignificant to be called stressful events but can accumulate and build up in people almost like electric charges stored in a battery. It has been found that people often have frequent episodes of subacute stress in the months before a heart attack or sudden cardiac death.

6. *Acute life stress*. By *acute*, we mean sudden, severe, and abrupt—in contrast to *chronic*, meaning of long duration and frequent recurrence. Bereavement is the acute life stress possessing the strongest impact, especially for women, who have two to three times greater

risk of cardiac death than men. Earthquakes and terrorist attacks are other sources of acute life stress that have been linked to cardiac-related deaths. People can literally die from fright during a major earth-quake, such as the 1994 California earthquake, in which there were twenty-four such deaths. As a result, the psychological health ramifications of the September 11, 2001, terrorist events surely will be the focus of future research.

7. *Panic attacks and panic disorder.* By *panic attacks* or *disorder* here we mean periods of intense apprehension or fear. During a panic attack, a person may complain of palpitations, chest pain, labored breathing or difficulty in breathing, fatigue, light-headedness, dizziness, and near or actual fainting. The chest pain from a panic attack can be difficult to differentiate from angina or a real heart attack. Interestingly, many patients with panic disorder also suffer from mitral valve prolapse (a malfunction of the valve between the upper and lower chamber on the heart's left side), and many cardiologists believe there is an association.

8. *Daily and seasonal rhythms.* This conspirator differs greatly from all the others in that it is not an emotion. However, daily and seasonal rhythms, which are mediated by an internal clock located in the brain, have specific effects on our emotions that can, in turn, become stressors and adversely affect our heart and circulatory system. Heart attacks are most frequent between 5:00 A.M. and 12:00 P.M. A high level of sympathetic nervous system activity and a high cortisol level (both of which are stimulated by the brain) between these hours are suspected to play an important role. The incidence of cardiac events peaks in fall and winter and is at its lowest point in summer. The same is true for the incidence of one type of depression called *seasonal affective disorder* (SAD). SAD emerges in the fall or winter months, and recovery occurs during spring and summer. Researchers suspect that there is a relationship between the high incidence of depression in the winter and the high number of cardiac events. Holidays are also considered to be stressors, and some of the biggest holidays of the year fall during the winter. The physical stress of winter low temperatures may also be a factor. All of these stressors can precipitate a heart attack and heart rhythm disturbances.

In our book, we investigate all eight of these heart-mind conspirators and check out what real dangers they pose to your heart and cardiovascular health. We show you what you can do to prevent trouble from developing, and we explain what you can do to alleviate and cure a problem when one does develop. We present the latest medications that are available and discuss how to minimize side effects and drug interactions.

How This Book Can Help You

Once you have identified your risk factors, what can you do if you find yourself in cardiac danger from one of the eight heart-mind conspirators? In real life, we have seen that it can take a combination of physicians with different medical backgrounds and training to help a person with cardiac trouble to fully recover. To put it simply, heart doctors and mind/brain doctors can learn from working with one another, and you can be the beneficiary.

However, you shouldn't expect to have your emotions taken into consideration when you seek treatment for a heart problem. Perhaps that is why you are reading this book. Use it to empower you to communicate with your doctor. Keep reading, and if you meet resistance or lack of understanding when you deal with your doctor, it's time you consider seeing someone else.

2

Heart Disease

When the Heart's in Trouble

CORONARY ARTERY DISEASE is one of the most frequent forms of cardiovascular disease. Hypertension (high blood pressure), stroke, and vascular disease are other common kinds. In order to better understand how depression and the other heart-mind conspirators are linked, it is important to understand how heart disease develops and what happens during a heart attack or bypass surgery. This chapter provides an overview and then leads you to the next few chapters, where you will find out how depression is linked to heart disease and how depression affects recovery from a heart attack or bypass surgery.

Touring the Heart and Circulatory System

The cardiovascular or circulatory system is made up of the heart, blood, and a network of blood vessels not unlike a highway system. The blood, pumped by the heart and oxygenated by the lungs, carries the oxygen to tissues all over the body through the arteries and returns to the heart by way of the veins.

Arteries have thicker walls than veins. The big pipe emerging near the top of the heart is the aorta, by far the largest of all arteries. The coronary arteries emerge at the base of the aorta, run along the surface of the heart, and carry oxygen to the heart itself, which is almost completely muscle tissue. Like any other body tissue, the heart muscle must be supplied with oxygen and nutrients by the blood. Its oxygen demands are high, because of its nonstop activity.

If anything interferes with the blood supply of oxygen to heart muscle, its pumping action is likely to malfunction. Coronary artery disease can interfere with the blood supply of oxygen to heart muscle, with a number of possible consequences, one of which is a heart attack.

As seen in Figure 2.1, the heart has four chambers, two upper (atria) and two lower (ventricles). The upper and lower chambers are connected, but in a normal heart, there are no sideways connections. The right side of the heart pumps oxygen-poor blood, and the left side pumps oxygen-rich blood. In this way, the heart manages to do two jobs at one time—pump left-ventricle blood through the body and operate a second smaller circulation system between the heart's right ventricle and the lungs. Oxygen-poor blood returns from body tissues through the veins. Two large veins, the superior vena cava and inferior vena cava, carry it into the heart. The oxygen-poor blood enters the right atrium (upper chamber). It passes through a valve into the right ventricle (lower chamber). From there it goes to the lungs.

Figure 2.1

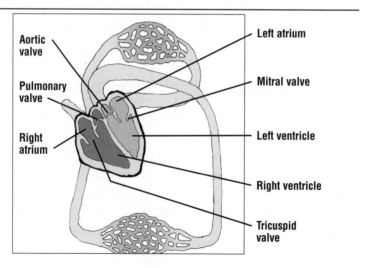

A diagram of the heart and circulatory system.

Blood is oxygenated within the lung (in tiny air sacs called *alveoli*) through contact with the air we breathe. The oxygenated blood returns to the heart. It enters the left atrium and passes down into the left ventricle. The oxygenated blood leaves the heart through the aorta, on its way to arteries all over the body. One of the shortest journeys is through the coronary arteries. There are two major coronary arteries on the heart: the right coronary artery and the left coronary artery, which supply several smaller arteries on the surface of the heart.

Coronary Artery Disease (Heart Disease)

While you may have learned about the heart and circulatory system, what many people do not know is how well our cardiovascular system is engineered. The heart beats, for most people, around seventy times a minute. That is more than four thousand times an hour, one hundred thousand times in twenty-four hours, and seven hundred thousand in just one week! After seventy years, the total number of heartbeats is difficult to count. The heart can keep going during an entire lifetime without ever needing an oil change or a tune-up. However, if your heart stalls for even a few minutes, you die.

Coronary artery disease, also known as *coronary heart disease*, consists of the buildup of plaque (fatty material) on the interior walls of the coronary arteries, a process called *atherosclerosis*. Its consequence may be ischemic heart disease, and angina, or chest pain, may be the first symptom. Unfortunately, a heart attack(a *myocardial infarction*)—particularly in men—may also be the first symptom of coronary artery disease.

Atherosclerosis: How Plaque Builds Up and Heart Disease Develops

Coronary artery disease begins with an initial injury to the vessel lining (endothelium) followed by plaque development, a process that occurs over many years. (In contrast, heart attacks usually result from the rupture of a plaque followed by clot formation, a process that takes minutes to hours.) Doctors are not sure of all the reasons why a blood clot forms on a plaque. The following steps are involved:

1. Plaque forms in the artery, a process that takes years or even decades.
2. An increase in blood flow or turbulence occurs across the plaque. Elevated blood pressure, stress, smoking, adrenaline, and many other conditions can bring about these blood flow changes.
3. An injury or rupture of the plaque is caused by the changes in blood flow. The plaque, having been damaged, provides a raw surface for platelets—the blood element that forms a clot—to stick.
4. An increase in the "stickiness" of the platelets occurs, and the blood clot forms. Stress hormones in the body have been shown to make platelets stickier. The importance of platelets in coronary artery disease is underscored by the near universal use of aspirin and other antiplatelet agents in heart disease.
5. When plaque ruptures, blood comes in contact with the fatty material and a clot forms. If the plaque and clot are very small, you may not have any symptoms. If the clot is large enough to block blood flow through the artery, you will have a heart attack.
6. Beyond the blockage point of the artery, the blood vessel branches and further microscopic vessels that oxygenate the heart muscle are deprived of blood, so the heart muscle cells in the part fed by the blocked artery begin to die. Generally, the heart muscle cells start to die about twenty to thirty minutes after the blockage occurs. If blood flow is not restored to that part of the heart within three hours, about 90 percent of the cells starved of blood are likely to die. This is the window of opportunity for reviving the heart muscle cells.

Why Plaque Builds Up in the First Place

Physicians investigating the cause of coronary artery disease have to ask themselves why plaque builds up on the interior wall at a particular place. What materials from the blood go into forming plaque?

What causes plaque to develop inside arteries? While there are answers to these questions, not everything in the explanations is known with certainty. In the media, cholesterol gets most of the blame. While it is certainly involved, cholesterol is not the only culprit. We know that some people with high blood levels of cholesterol never develop heart trouble. In fact, a significant percentage of people who suffer heart attacks have normal blood cholesterol levels. Clearly, then, other factors are involved.

Plaque buildup is not a simple mechanical process, like deposits building up inside a drainage pipe until it gets clogged. Instead, plaque is thought to first build up at the site of an injury to the artery's interior wall. Just as turbulent water erodes a stream's banks at certain places, turbulences in blood flow can injure the delicate cells that line the artery wall. This is particularly likely to happen at artery branches and especially in people with high blood pressure. Substances traveling in the bloodstream (such as microorganisms), substances secreted by the immune system, substances that contract and dilate blood vessels, and toxic chemicals may further injure these cells. High blood pressure and high levels of insulin may also damage the endothelial cells lining the coronary arteries.

The plaque-buildup process is thought to begin with three steps:

1. The cells lining the artery wall permit fatty particles to penetrate into the wall.
2. Adhesion molecules cling to the artery wall at certain places, attracting white blood cells and modified LDL (bad cholesterol) particles.
3. The LDL particles enable white blood cells to enter the artery wall.

This is the beginning of an inflammatory process. The damaged endothelial lining continues to attract white blood cells, many of which are monocytes (white blood cells that prey on foreign substances). Monocytes turn into large scavenger cells called macrophages, which attract more LDL. The LDL particles become oxidized by oxygen-free radicals as they infiltrate the artery wall. When macrophages engulf

LDL cholesterol, they become foam cells. Foam cells gather in fatty streaks in the artery wall.

The macrophages also release toxins that magnify the damage to the arterial inner wall. This additional injury causes more platelets to adhere. The platelets and macrophages may induce smooth muscle cells in the vessel wall to encapsulate the debris, which by now includes particles of calcium and lipid as well as cells. This buildup of cells and debris is plaque. Obstruction of blood flow depends on the size of the plaque.

How Atherosclerosis Progresses

Atherosclerosis is now seen as a process of chronic inflammation. In a healthy inflammation process, such as when you cut yourself, white blood cells rush to the injury site to fight bacterial invaders, and fibrinogen enables the blood to clot so that you do not bleed to death. In atherosclerosis, this healthy process has gone wrong. The white blood cells interact with the artery wall instead of with foreign invaders, and fibrinogen, a protein produced by the liver, helps form a clot that blocks blood flow through the artery. Inflammatory markers, like C-reactive protein, can signal, through high levels in the blood, that an inflammatory process is taking place somewhere in the body.

The process of atherosclerosis is slow, perhaps over decades. It's generally believed that many men develop atherosclerosis during their thirties and forties, possibly at an even earlier age, which progresses into coronary artery disease in their fifties or sixties. Men in their twenties have been found on autopsy to have atherosclerosis, demonstrating that the process begins at a relatively young age. The female hormone estrogen seems to protect women from atherosclerosis until menopause, around the age of fifty. This gives women a delay of about ten years in developing atherosclerosis. However, they do catch up. Women in high-stress jobs and those juggling family and career may be more vulnerable to atherosclerosis. There is evidence to suggest that women are more likely to die from their heart attack than men. Additionally, children as young as ten have been found to have atherosclerosis. This is suspected to be caused by junk food and a sedentary lifestyle.

Angina: An Important Warning Sign and Symptom of Heart Disease

Angina, the chest pain caused by insufficient arterial blood flow to the heart muscles, is the most frequent symptom of coronary artery disease. It's also a frightening and misleading symptom. It's frightening because some people who feel chest pain are afraid of having a heart attack, and others assume they are having a heart attack. It is misleading because chest pain can indeed be caused by indigestion. It can also be caused by anxiety, a panic attack, and gallbladder disease as well as a heart attack.

The absence of angina pain or other symptoms in the presence of ischemic heart disease (that is, reduced blood flow to the heart) is called *silent ischemia*. This can be a dangerous condition in that atherosclerotic disease may progress to major coronary artery blockage without warning.

Symptoms of Angina

The chest pain of angina varies with individuals. The textbook angina is a left-sided chest pain that goes to the left arm or jaw, but angina can be on the right chest, back, or even in the abdomen. The pain can be sharp, dull, burning, or pressure-like. Angina can also be felt as a shortness of breath, a condition often called *angina equivalent.*

Some people have angina only when they physically exert themselves, which usually indicates that a coronary artery has a significant blockage. A meal, cold weather, or stress can also bring on angina. However, some people feel chest pain even when they are at rest, which generally means that a coronary artery is severely obstructed.

Types of Angina

Unstable angina is the term given to chest pain that is either new or becoming progressively more severe and occurring more readily and with less physical effort. For example, a man who develops angina after walking for three city blocks and has been this way for several years has stable angina. However, if he starts to develop angina after walking only one city block, he now has unstable angina. Unstable angina is usually a more significant warning sign than stable angina, signaling a progression of coronary artery disease; that is, greater obstruction of blood flow through one or more coronary arteries. Both stable and unstable angina require further diagnosis and intervention. The recommended treatment, ranging from medications to surgery, depends on the location of the blockage, the severity of blockage, how many vessels are affected, and the symptoms.

Spasms of the coronary arteries can also cause angina. This kind of angina is more prevalent in women than in men. In a spasm, the blood flow is restricted by a contraction of the artery, which is usually temporary. Spasms seem to occur more often in arteries that already have plaque buildup. Over the years, I have seen many patients with classical angina whose evaluation for heart disease turned out to be negative. I believe many of them had coronary spasm.

Risk Factors for Coronary Artery Disease

These days everyone seems to know the risk factors for coronary artery disease. But do we really? The risk factors as we know them were recently reviewed by researchers at the University of Miami. First and foremost, as proven direct causes, they ranked:

- Cigarette smoking
- High blood cholesterol levels
- High blood pressure
- Advancing age

A second group consists of risk factors that have not been proved to be direct causes of coronary artery disease but have been shown without doubt to be associated with it. These are the so-called conditional risk factors:

- High blood triglyceride levels. Most of your body fat is stored as triglycerides, a lipid. Triglycerides also circulate in the blood, making it possible to measure their level.
- Coagulation factors. A substance that assists blood clotting, such as fibrinogen, can help promote a clot on ruptured plaque inside an artery.

- Certain lipoproteins. Lipoproteins are mixtures of lipid and protein, some of which are inflammatory markers.
- Homocysteine. This substance is believed to attack the artery wall.

The third group covers the predisposing risk factors, which probably influence and interact with the first and second groups of risk factors. They include the following, not ranked in order of potency or importance:

- Obesity
- Sedentary lifestyle
- Family history of coronary artery disease
- Male gender
- Insulin resistance
- Psychosocial factors

The University of Miami researchers include psychosocial factors (which we mentioned briefly in Chapter 1) in the third group because they regard the scientific evidence linking them to coronary artery disease to be less strong than, say, cigarette smoking. While psychosocial factors are often ranked at the very end or not mentioned at all, we believe that they are very important risk factors and should be ranked much higher. For example, it has been shown under laboratory conditions that mental stress rivals physical exercise in its ability to cause ischemic changes in subjects with coronary artery disease.

With risk factors in general, do not expect simple cause-and-effect relationships between them and diseases. Usually risk factors do not occur alone in an individual. When they coexist, they can interrelate with one another, gaining potency.

Another complication is individual variability—what affects one person may have little or no effect on another. We all know stories of people who smoked heavily all their lives without health consequences. Such people either are blessed with certain protective genes or lack genes that promote development of specific disease. Some people are just lucky. Most of us know that risk factors usually don't condemn you to developing a disorder. When you make changes in the way you live, you can eliminate some risk factors. The ones you can't get rid of, you can often lessen by taking a little extra care. For this reason, coronary artery disease is usually a preventable disorder.

Heart Attack: When Heart Disease Goes Unnoticed

Nearly a million Americans a year have a heart attack. Getting to the hospital for quick treatment is one of the keys to survival after a heart attack. More than nine out of ten heart attack victims who arrive at the hospital in time for something to be done for them survive. Physician experience and the sophisticated techniques, equipment, and medications available at American hospitals are responsible for this very high survival rate. Currently doctors are striving to improve the survival rate of patients after leaving the hospital following a heart attack.

What Happens During a Heart Attack

Doctors refer to a heart attack as an *acute myocardial infarction*. The myocardium is the heart muscle, and an infarct is an area of necrosis (dead tissue) caused by a lack of blood supply. A heart attack is the cardiac event that everyone dreads and tries to prevent. In a heart attack, the blood supply is cut off completely and suddenly, and heart muscles begin to die from the lack of oxygen.

Unlike most other cells in the body, heart muscles cannot regrow. Once the heart muscles die, the area is eventually replaced with scar tissue, permanently damaging the pump function of the heart.

Recognizing Symptoms and Warning Signs

Heart attack pain varies. Characteristically, it is a crushing chest pain. You may also be sweating or dizzy or feel weak or short of breath. If the pain lasts longer than twenty to thirty minutes and is not eased by rest, it may be a heart attack; seek emergency help. Although angina usually comes on with exertion and improves with rest, this is not the case with heart attack.

How does the pain from angina differ from that of a heart attack? Sometimes they are not easy to tell apart. Pain from a heart attack is generally more severe than angina. People who have been through a heart attack describe it as a severe crushing chest pain. Others describe it more as chest pressure, heartburn, or back pain. Some heart attack patients don't experience any pain at all, and this is called a silent MI. Not feeling well, tiredness, light-headedness, sweating, and shortness of breath are some other symptoms of heart attacks.

A heart attack can also really feel like indigestion, though this happens less often than these other symptoms. You feel a dull ache in your upper stomach. You may also feel weak or as if you are about to faint.

People have heart attacks most often in the early morning, between the hours of 5:00 and noon. In cold climates, people are more likely to have a heart attack in the fall or winter. We discuss this topic more in Chapter 12 with our discussion of daily and seasonal rhythms.

It should come as no surprise that most heart attacks are caused by coronary heart disease. In turn, depression and the other heart-mind conspirators play a much greater role in causing coronary artery disease than is widely known, which we talk about in greater detail in Chapter 4.

Bypass Surgery:
Preventing a Possible Heart Attack

Coronary bypass surgery is generally recommended for people who have significant narrowing (stenosis) of their coronary arteries, those with unstable angina or angina sufficiently severe to interfere with daily life, and those who had been treated unsuccessfully by other means. The operation can prolong life, avoid a heart attack, and relieve chest pain. Many people are unaware that improvement in quality of life is an important goal of coronary bypass surgery.

According to the American Heart Association, about seven hundred thousand open-heart operations were performed in the United States in 1998. Among these procedures, coronary bypass operations were the most frequent, making up more than five hundred thousand. Of the remaining operations, ninety thousand were heart valve procedures, another ninety thousand were for congenital heart conditions and so forth, and slightly more than two thousand were heart transplants.

What Is Bypassed in Bypass Surgery?

One of the first successful coronary artery bypass operations was performed by Drs. Michael DeBakey and Antonio Gotto at the Methodist Hospital in Houston, Texas, in 1964. The patient was a forty-two-year-old man with severe incapacitating angina. Even though many technical advances have been made since the early 1960s, the coronary bypass operations that surgeons perform today bear many similarities to the early operations.

Before any operation, surgeons need a coronary arteriogram to locate the obstructing plaques inside the coronary arteries. Coronary arteriograms are made by injecting a dye into the coronary arteries and following its progress on a television monitor. Obstructing plaque shows on an arteriogram like an aerial view of a sandbar in a river. With coronary arteriograms, surgeons can figure out ways to get arterial blood directly from the heart's aorta to branches of the coronary arteries being deprived of blood by plaque obstructions. In other words, surgeons bypass the obstruction.

To make a bypass around an obstruction in a coronary artery, a blood vessel is taken from another part of the patient and then grafted at one end to the aorta. The surgeon then grafts the other end to the coronary artery at a point beyond the plaque obstruction. Thus arterial blood can flow freely from the heart's aorta through the grafted blood vessel into the branches of the coronary artery, feeding the heart muscle oxygen and nutrients. This procedure, known as CABG (yes, cabbage) for coronary artery bypass grafting, has become so familiar, people usually refer to it simply as a *bypass*. Figure 2.2 shows a double coronary artery bypass operation. A triple bypass means that three blocked arteries in the heart were bypassed. Former president Clinton recently had a quadruple, or four-vessel, bypass.

A segment of the saphenous vein, a fairly large vein near the surface of the leg, is often used to bypass a blockage in the right coronary artery (as seen in Figure 2.2). Loss of this vein from the leg causes no problems in blood circulation, because there are sufficient substitute veins in the leg. A vein is not an ideal substitute for an artery, however, because veins often become gradually obstructed themselves. At least one-third to one-half of vein bypasses fail in ten years or fewer, which means another coronary bypass operation may be necessary.

Use of an artery rather than a vein as a bypass is more long lasting. The left internal mammary artery is usually selected, but the right can also be used. This artery branches off the subclavian artery and runs along the lateral part of the breastbone. In contrast to vein grafts, approximately 90 percent of mammary artery grafts are still open in ten years.

Figure 2.2 Blockage in the Right Coronary Artery

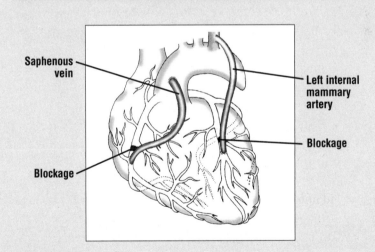

A saphenous vein is used to bypass a blockage in the right coronary artery.

We hope that you now have an understanding of how heart disease forms and the warning signs and surgery used to stop a heart attack from developing. Our concern—and the reason for writing this book—is that doctors and patients do not take psychosocial cardiac risk factors as seriously as they do physical risk factors. It is very important to deal with cigarette smoking or a high blood cholesterol level, but it is also important to deal with emotional stressors. If you don't take a risk factor seriously, you probably won't make much effort to eliminate it or reduce its effectiveness. This is what's happening in America today, and it's what we hope to change in the following chapters.

3

The Poison Fog
of Depression

WILLIAM STYRON, AUTHOR OF *Sophie's Choice* and an account of his own depression, *Darkness Visible*, described his depression as a poison fog that rolled in upon his mind at about 3:00 every afternoon. He had to lie in bed, often for as long as six hours, waiting for it to lift mysteriously.

Depression is a silent disease of the mind. It is also a silent killer. The links between depression and heart disease are undeniable, yet depression is often undiagnosed and untreated. An important step toward cardiovascular health for many heart patients is having a basic understanding of depression, discussed in this chapter.

Who Gets Depressed?

At least seventeen and a half million American adults suffer from depression at some time each year. One in ten people are affected, with a depressed person in one out of every five families. Nearly two-thirds of depressed people don't realize they have the condition. Among those who do know, some are ashamed, seeing depression as personal weakness or a character flaw; relatively few receive adequate treatment. Because of the large numbers of undiagnosed and untreated sufferers, some experts consider these estimates to be too low. In addition, about 15 percent of people are affected by depression at some point in their lives, though people are most likely to suffer from it in middle age. In developed countries, depression ranks second, just behind coronary artery disease, as the major cause of early death and disability.

Some people hide their depression well. They can, for example, hold highly demanding jobs during working hours, but when they are home alone, they feel severely depressed and become almost incapacitated. Finding pleasure in nothing, they have little appetite for food, and sleeping is a problem. They don't socialize, and some don't even want to talk on the phone. They may sit in front of the television for the entire evening without really watching anything. Some stare at a book without taking in what they read. A few just sleep the whole evening away. The next morning, they pack away their depression and try to put on a cheerful and friendly front for another day at their jobs. This can go on for some time until coping mechanisms collapse.

Depression in the Elderly

Depression in people over sixty-five is especially difficult. The disability is more debilitating and the diminished quality of life more pronounced. It frequently places challenging demands on family members and caregivers. Of more than thirty million Americans who are sixty-five or older, at least five million (the actual number is likely much higher) have documented depressive symptoms, but very few of these individuals are getting any treatment at all.

Researchers at the University of Pennsylvania School of Medicine pointed out that depression in older people may be different in essential ways from that in younger people. There's much about older people's depression that is not fully understood. For example, their depression is frequently manifested as physical symptoms and is, therefore, easily mistaken as a medical illness. Thus, an elderly person's only symptom might be something that could readily be attributed to the infirmities of age rather than emotional state.

In addition, elderly patients are treated mostly in the offices of primary care physicians, who tend to their physical ailments. Because many older patients don't usually present with depressed mood, they are less frequently referred by their doctors to mental health specialists. For example, a doctor treating an elderly person for chest pain would have no reason to suspect that it might be associated with depression if the patient never mentioned feeling low. Doctors naturally expect elderly people to have some physical infirmities, so unless somehow alerted, they do not have the same expectation of emotional disorders.

Women and Depression

Women are twice as likely as men to be diagnosed with depression. Although young boys and girls have an equal risk of depression during childhood, during adolescence, more girls than boys become depressed. This increased incidence of depression continues through a woman's life into old age. Of American women, 10 to 25 percent have major depression at some point of their lives. Of American men, the number is 7 to 12 percent.

There are several possible explanations for why women are more prone to depression than men are. Some women may respond to life stress differently on a genetic basis. Others may actually have more stress. The modern woman's roles in both workplace and home are likely to involve distressful worries and conflicts.

On the other hand, women may be more frequently diagnosed with depression because they are more willing than men to seek medical help. They are also more willing than men to acknowledge their feelings. Men tend to repress the symptoms of their depression (doctors use the term *alexithymia* for the condition of finding it hard to express your emotional state in words). The symptoms of a man's mood disorder may also be masked by his alcohol or drug abuse. Doctors diagnose the substance abuse but not the depression beneath. In fact, in some communities where alcohol and street drugs are not readily available, men and women are diagnosed with depression with more or less equal frequency.

The emotional downs that women experience due to hormonal shifts during their menstrual cycles may be associated with depression. The hormonal changes of pregnancy and childbirth may also precipitate mood changes. Although depression has been traditionally viewed as a symptom of menopause, it's now understood that many women don't become clinically depressed at that time; and typically those who do have had previous episodes of depression.

Destigmatizing Depression

Back in February of 1976, President Jimmy Carter established a President's Commission on Mental Health, with Rosalynn Carter as honorary chairperson. The commission worked hard to improve community mental health and had some success in raising the profile of mental health in this country. A particular focus was placed on the problems of stigma and discrimination. Almost thirty years later, at her Mental Health Program at the Carter Center, Mrs. Carter continues to work valiantly to eliminate the stigma of mental illness. That progress is being made in reducing this stigma is a testimony to her work and the work of other advocates in organizations such as the National Mental Health Association and National Alliance for the Mentally Ill. The first ever U.S. surgeon general's report on mental health, issued in 1999, made clear that mental illnesses like depression have a physical basis and are diagnosable and treatable. This report has had a positive effect in reducing the stigma of mental illness.

In this context, prominent people are becoming more candid about having been depressed. Congressman Patrick Kennedy has discussed his depression publicly. Tipper Gore, wife of former vice president Al Gore, has spoken openly about receiving treatment for major depression after a car accident that nearly took the life of her young son. The entire Gore family received counseling after the incident. Mrs. Gore and former secretary of state Colin Powell's wife, Alma, have been active in the National Mental Health Awareness Campaign, which has the goal of reducing the stigma surrounding diseases such as depression.

In addition, novelist William Styron, humorist Art Buch-
wald, and TV journalists Mike Wallace and Jane Pauley have
been eloquent about their struggles with mood disorders.
Actors Rod Steiger, Carrie Fisher, and Margot Kidder have
been open in discussing their mental illnesses. All are to be
commended for their courage in coming forward to relieve the
suffering of their fellow human beings.

Perhaps the most powerful testimony comes to us from the
Civil War era. Historians now believe that Abraham Lincoln
suffered from major depression, or *melancholia*, as it was then
known. His achievements can inspire those who struggle with
depression during their lives.

Recognizing Depression

If you don't have any symptoms of depression yourself, you may recognize them in a family member or friend. The following sections sort
out the distinctions among normal sadness, minor depression, and the
varied symptoms of major depression.

How Do I Know Whether My Sorrow Is Normal?

When something bad happens to you, it is normal to feel sad. We all
have events in our lives that cause us to feel sad, such as bereavement, divorce, or loss of work. Under these circumstances, sadness
is a healthy reaction. Although your sad feelings may be intense, you
carry on with your life in spite of them. As time passes, your dejec-
tion eases.

The unexpected death of someone you love is the hardest news to
bear. You may refuse to accept that your child, husband, wife, parent,
sibling, or friend has died, although you go through the motions of
attending the funeral or whatever else family and friends expect of you.
All of it feels unreal. After a short time, the loss of your loved one
becomes painfully real to you and your sorrow can grow intense. You

may feel despair, guilt, and bewilderment. It is during this phase that you are most likely to show depressive symptoms. But often, sorrow becomes more bearable with time, and once more you begin to notice people and things around you. You still mourn the loss of your loved one. But in spite of that, you find yourself looking forward to something and smiling at a joke.

You do not have a mood disorder.

Without setting absolute time limits, doctors estimate that two months of deep sorrow is normal and healthy. Beyond two months, your mood should be starting to improve. Many psychiatrists now believe that if significant depressive symptoms persist in grief-stricken patients six months or so after their loss, they should seek professional help.

Recognizing Minor Depression

Minor depression, as defined by many medical researchers, is depression in which the symptoms are not quite severe enough to qualify as major depression (discussed in the following section). The condition of long-term gloominess that psychiatrists refer to as *dysthymia* is also sometimes called minor depression and fits within our use of the terms.

But don't think of minor depression as a "minor" problem, particularly not in older people. The depressive symptoms of minor depression have been associated with physical illness, functional impairment, and death; and many people with minor depression go on to develop major depression.

Dysphoria (also called *melancholia* and a *low mood*) can be so overwhelming that you may not even remember what it was like to feel otherwise. In a depressed mood, you may resent advice or assistance. Your unpleasant demeanor may drive people away, and you can become increasingly socially isolated as your condition worsens. Caught in a quicksand of despair, you may not be able to free yourself or reach out for help.

Being contentious, refusing to "look on the bright side of things," and being hard-nosed about what you perceive as reality does not mean that you have minor depression. But when your melancholy, bad mood, sadness, or loss of interest is prolonged, seek professional help.

Statistics to Keep in Mind

Depression at the level of a mood disorder requires professional care. However, while your depression may lift without professional care, note these statistics of people not receiving treatment:

- Of one hundred who have had one episode of depression, fifty will have another.
- Of one hundred who have had two episodes of depression, seventy will have another.
- Of one hundred who have had three episodes of depression, ninety will have another.

Major depression is the main cause of suicide, accounting for up to 35 percent of approximately thirty thousand suicides per year. However, while most people realize that untreated depression can lead to suicide, and some are aware that depression can result in alcohol and substance abuse, virtually no one knows that depression is a risk factor for coronary artery disease and sudden cardiac death.

When Your Symptoms Point to Major Depression

When your feelings of sadness don't lift with time and begin to interfere with your work and social relationships, you may be developing major depression, also known as *clinical depression, unipolar depression*, or *major depressive disorder*. There is no lab test to show that you have major depression. A doctor cannot tell by examining your eyes or skin or listening to your heartbeat. Instead, he or she relies on the presence of certain symptoms to make a diagnosis. These symptoms are of four kinds:

- Mood
- Behavior

- Thinking
- Physical symptoms

Symptoms vary with personality. They also may vary with age. For example, the most noticeable symptom in depressed young people is often a change in behavior; in the middle-aged, a low mood; and in the elderly, something physical.

Some people also feel better and worse at different times of the day. Those with major depression often feel worse in the early morning and better later in the day. This can distinguish them from people with other debilitating diseases who, in contrast, start the day with more energy but feel worse as the day wears on. But every person is different, and women may have increased depression in the days before menstruation.

When diagnosing depression, doctors look for at least five of the following nine symptoms:

1. Dysphoria (a depressed mood or loss of interest). This symptom must be predominant. It must be at least two weeks duration, with depressed mood every day for most of the day, and severe enough to interfere with daily life, such as job performance or relations with family and friends.

The other eight symptoms consist of:

2. Sleep disturbance
3. Loss of interest or pleasure in things previously enjoyed
4. Feelings of guilt, hopelessness, helplessness, or worthlessness
5. Energy loss or fatigue
6. Concentration difficulties
7. Appetite decrease or increase
8. Psychomotor retardation or agitation (slow or agitated movement)
9. Suicidal thinking

Doctors use the mnemonic—developed by Carey Gross, a former Massachusetts General Hospital (MGH) psychiatrist—"SIG: E CAPS," reminiscent of a prescription, to remember the last eight of the symptoms, with *S* for sleep, *I* for interest, *G* for guilt, *E* for energy, *C* for concentration, *A* for appetite, *P* for psychomotor change, and *S* for suicidality.

Because depression clouds judgment, your assessment of your own symptoms may not be reliable. If you think you have major depression, ask your family members or friends whether they have noticed the symptoms. If your symptoms indicate major depression, seek professional help.

Minor Depression

The first symptom, dysphoria or minor depression, previously discussed as a depressed mood or loss of interest, must be predominant. This symptom must be of at least two weeks duration and severe enough to interfere with your daily life—as in job performance or relations with family and friends.

Sleep Disturbance

Four out of five people with major depression have trouble sleeping. Some find it hard to fall asleep after going to bed. Others wake during the night and remain awake, going over their troubles in their minds. Awakening before dawn (early-morning awakening) is a frequent complaint—for some, a sign of approaching depression. A smaller number of depressed people escape into long periods of sleep.

Loss of Interest or Pleasure in Things Previously Enjoyed

Normally, you may take pleasure in taking a walk in the park, having a clean home, reading a newspaper, watching a TV show, or making a long phone call to a friend. These small things add zest to your life. Without them, your free time could be monotonous. But when you experience depression, you may stop enjoying these pleasures. Friends may notice your loss of interest or pleasure in them but see no significance in it. Loss of interest in family is more liable to be commented on. Your apathy may also include loss of pleasure in sex. In fact, a diminishment in sex drive is frequently a warning of oncoming depression.

Feelings of Guilt, Hopelessness, Helplessness, or Worthlessness

The guilt involved in depression is not self-reproach about feeling sad and being a party pooper. It's excessive or inappropriate guilt and can even be delusional. Excessive feelings of guilt, hopelessness, or worthlessness can further isolate you.

Energy Loss or Fatigue

You're likely to feel tired much of the time when you are depressed. You feel you don't have enough energy to perform everyday tasks that you once did without thinking about it. Your work performance declines, your home goes uncleaned, and anything that requires effort on your part gets postponed.

Concentration Difficulties

Depression can cause difficulties in concentrating, thinking logically, or making decisions. You may also suffer from memory loss. Depression can affect your judgment, so that you may find yourself at a loss to explain why you did something.

Appetite Decrease or Increase

Some people find depression a highly effective—though highly unpleasant and maladaptive—way to lose weight. That's because, when depressed, you may lose your appetite. You may hardly notice food anymore, or you may be almost nauseated by the thought of it. To count as a depressive symptom, your loss of appetite should have accounted for more than a 5 percent loss of body weight in a month while you were not on a diet. Other depressed people gain significant amounts of weight through increased appetite. They may also have cravings for sugar and simple carbohydrates, such as cake.

Psychomotor Retardation or Agitation (Slow or Agitated Movement)

Depression can slow down your movements. You may speak very slowly and take a long time to respond to what is said to you. People may notice you sighing. You may walk around with your shoulders slumped and your eyes on the ground, avoiding eye contact with people. But you can't rely on self-assessment for this, because you may be only imagining you have slowed down. Others need to have noticed it, too.

The opposite is agitated movement: you may not be able to sit still, you may be constantly walking up and down, or you may wring your hands and gesture nervously. Older people are more likely than the young to develop agitated movements.

Suicidal Thinking

Planning to commit suicide is the negative extreme of depressive thinking. If you are making plans, tell your family and friends about them as soon as possible. Even thinking about suicide a lot but without making plans is still a reason to seek professional help without delay. Preoccupation with thoughts of death, but not merely fear of it, is part of this symptom. About two-thirds of people with major depression consider suicide, and major depression is the most frequent underlying illness in the five hundred thousand people who visit emergency rooms each year after suicide attempts.

Fifteen out of a hundred people with suicidal thoughts eventually commit suicide, as compared to one out of a hundred people who do not regularly have suicidal thoughts. Ironically, a number of people say they would have committed suicide had they not been too depressed to make the effort. Doctors in clinics need to closely monitor some depressed patients with reduced psychomotor activity when they receive antidepressants in the early stages of treatment. This is because antidepressants may restore energy to the patients before relieving their depression. As a result, patients may have enough energy to enact and carry through on a suicide plan.

Other Symptoms of Depression

In addition to these nine symptoms, there are other important ones that can signify depression.

- Feeling anxious
- Experiencing self-loathing
- Thinking you can't be helped

- Experiencing highs as well as lows (this may reflect a condition known as *manic depression* or *bipolar disorder*—see Experiencing Mania below)
- Experiencing physical ailments and pain

Feeling Anxious

Nine out of ten people with major depression suffer from anxiety, feeling apprehension or fear for some impending threat they haven't yet perceived. They feel something is going to happen. Their heart races. They feel shortness of breath. They perspire. We will look at anxiety in Chapter 7.

Experiencing Self-Loathing

By magnifying your faults and minimizing your good qualities, you may come to believe that you are an awful person. A beautiful woman can become totally convinced that she is ugly. Such self-loathing is characteristic of major depression.

Thinking You Can't Be Helped

You may decide that your condition is so bad, you are beyond treatment. Frequently, depressed patients don't recognize that they are responding to treatment. They feel no sign of improvement or easing of symptoms, although their progress is already obvious to others.

Experiencing Mania

We've already mentioned that depression can interfere with your thinking process and cloud your judgment. This isn't limited to difficulty concentrating or feelings of inappropriate guilt or worthlessness. It can work the other way too—for instance, someone can become convinced that he or she has extraordinary powers. Those who experience abnormally elevated or elated moods have a condition called *mania*. Mania is an essential feature of bipolar disorder (often called *manic depression*), in which people have episodes of mania and depression. To distinguish it, doctors often refer to major depression as *unipolar depression*. Bipolar (or manic) depression has its own distinct characteristics and is outside the scope of this book, but there are many useful resources out there on this topic. *Manic Depressive Illness* by

Frederick Goodwin and Kay Jamison and *The Unquiet Mind* by Kay Jamison are two excellent books on the subject.

Experiencing Physical Ailments and Pain

You may also find yourself often complaining of physical ailments, particularly pain, headaches, and gastrointestinal problems. Depressed women may have irregular or painful menstrual periods.

The problem that arises from this situation is that when people seek remedies for their physical ailments, they often don't tell their doctors about their depression. When the remedy prescribed proves to be ineffectual, the doctor may be at a loss to explain why. Some people try a succession of prescription drugs—and a succession of doctors as well—in their vain efforts to find relief. Doctors often refer to these patients as *somatizers*, because their underlying distress is being expressed in physical symptoms. Most commonly, patients are relieved of their physical ailment through successful treatment of depression.

A Quick Depression Test

The Harvard Department of Psychiatry/National Depression Screening Day Scale (HANDS) is a self-administered test for depression and consists of this questionnaire. Use the following scale to answer each of these questions:

0 (None or little of the time)

1 (Some of the time)

2 (Most of the time)

3 (All of the time)

Over the past two weeks how often have you:

1. Been feeling low in energy, slowed down?
2. Been blaming yourself for things?

3. Had poor appetite?
4. Had difficulty falling asleep, staying asleep?
5. Been feeling hopeless about the future?
6. Been feeling blue?
7. Been feeling no interest in things?
8. Had thoughts of worthlessness?
9. Thought about or wanted to commit suicide?
10. Had difficulty concentrating or making decisions?

Now sum up your scores for the ten questions for a total score, and look at what the numbers may indicate.

0–8: Major depression is unlikely; an evaluation is not recommended.*

9–16: Major depression is likely; symptoms are consistent with major depressive disorder. A major depressive disorder evaluation is recommended.

17–30: Major depression is very likely; symptoms are strongly consistent with major depressive disorder. A major depressive disorder evaluation is strongly recommended for what is likely severe depression, requiring immediate attention.

*Scoring one point or more on question 9 on suicide requires an evaluation, regardless of total score on the HANDS. There may also be other reasons for evaluation, of course.

The HANDS™ Depression Screening Tool was developed by Screening for Mental Health, Inc. and the Department of Psychiatry, Harvard Medical School. Copyright © 1998, 2002 by Screening for Mental Health, Inc. and the President and Fellows of Harvard College. All rights reserved. Used by permission.

Finding Help for Depression

Insomnia, fatigue or lack of energy, concentration difficulties, and loss of appetite are frequent symptoms of depression. But many other medical problems can have exactly the same symptoms. Cancer, diabetes, thyroid disease, anemia, and neurological problems are some examples. Differentiating them from depression is not always an easy task. That is why professional help is important with both the evaluation and treatment.

The good news is that there are effective therapies for depression. But unless you ask for help or your family or friends intercede, your suffering from depression is likely to continue, and your overall health is likely to worsen.

Having practiced cardiac surgery for many years, I know many patients with heart disease also have problems with depression, both before and after an open-heart operation or a heart attack. I routinely raise the topic of depression with my patients and their families, and I provide an environment where psychiatric support is readily available. Psychiatrists like my coauthor are invaluable. These specialized doctors, through their expert evaluation and treatment, have improved the emotional and physical well-being of many heart patients. In Part III of this book, you'll find some strategies and suggestions for treating this chief heart-mind conspirator.

4

Depression's Link to Coronary Artery Disease

Margaret, a sixty-year-old landscape gardener in Atlanta, had been depressed on and off for years. But she had always managed to function at her work in the suburbs of the expanding city. Somewhat vague about her history of depression, she had been prescribed several antidepressants by different doctors over the years and claimed they had helped. However, as soon as she felt better, she would stop taking the medication. Margaret was single, feisty, and independent. She didn't believe in giving people much information about herself. Unfortunately, that included people who needed the information to evaluate her condition and recommend appropriate treatment.

She first felt a lingering dull pain deep in her chest when she made a major physical effort in her gardening work. When she rested, the pain faded away. Margaret attributed it to dinner from the previous night. She took some antacid tablets and went on with her work. Over the next few weeks, she tried to be more careful about her eating habits, but the pain often returned when she physically exerted herself. Finally, she saw her doctor about it. The doctor sent Margaret to a cardiologist.

After the results of tests came in, the cardiologist told her that she had angina pectoris (chest pain due to the heart not getting enough oxygen) caused by coronary artery disease. He told her that her pain—her angina—was a warning sign and that she needed to pay attention to these signs and make changes in her life if she wanted to avoid a heart attack.

Margaret didn't smoke or drink. She led an active life and had a normal blood cholesterol level. She had no idea why she should develop heart trouble and told the doctor so. The cardiologist agreed that apart from her coronary artery atherosclerosis, she was remarkably fit for a woman of sixty. On the basis of physical health, he admitted, she was right—she should not have heart trouble. But he noted the brief mention of antidepressants on the information sheet she had filled in. Margaret told him about her depressive episodes and mentioned also that she had frequently been under a lot of stress from her business. She was too busy to have friends, she claimed, and no longer spoke to family members because of money they had borrowed and not paid back. On top of this, she now recalled she had a family history of cardiac problems. The cardiologist listened as these cardiac risk factors appeared, one after another, in what had only minutes before seemed a bafflingly risk-free patient.

Margaret was fortunate to have seen a cardiologist who recognized these nonphysical cardiac risk factors and took them seriously. In addition to taking a prescription medicine for chest pain, she somewhat reluctantly agreed to see a psychiatrist. She soon realized that being physically and emotionally fit are both important for a healthy heart.

THAT DEPRESSION IS A potential cause or risk factor as well as a consequence of coronary artery disease represents a major change in how we look at heart disease. Up until recently, doctors have looked at depression primarily as a consequence of heart disease. This was a reasonable assumption as coronary artery disease is a chronic disease and can cause stress, pain, discomfort, disability, and other symptoms in varying degrees of severity. While depression has been linked to hypertension, stroke, arrhythmia, and other kinds of heart disease, in this chapter, we look mainly at the links between depression and coronary artery disease and the arrhythmias that often accompany it.

Depression as a Risk Factor for Coronary Artery Disease

Coronary artery disease is one of the most frequent forms of cardiovascular disease. High blood pressure (hypertension), stroke, and vascular disease are other common kinds. In general, I find that patients are generally quite knowledgeable about the causes of coronary artery disease. However, seldom is someone aware that depression is also a potential risk factor for coronary artery disease. Most are puzzled that such a causal relationship even exists, and many want more information.

Proving that depression is a cause of heart disease is not an easy task. Coronary artery disease takes many decades to develop. By the time you have chest pain, a heart attack, or other symptoms, the underlying coronary artery disease process has already progressed to an advanced stage. In order to show that depression is a cause, it would be helpful to go back to a time before symptoms began to show. But at this very early stage, coronary artery disease is difficult to diagnose, and it is nearly impossible to identify people who are affected. It also doesn't help that many depressed people don't seek help, and those who do are often unwilling to identify themselves.

However, the studies mentioned in the next few sections provide compelling evidence that depression is a risk factor for coronary artery disease and is responsible for more heart attacks and cardiac mortality. They serve as a warning that depression should be attended to because it has, among other effects, adverse health consequences on the heart.

Depressed Mood and Hopelessness

Depressed mood and hopelessness are two symptoms of depression, and there have been many studies linking coronary artery disease to these symptoms. One significant study involved researchers at the Centers for Disease Control and Prevention who traced the links between these two symptoms and ischemic heart disease in a study using data collected in the National Health Examination Follow-Up Study. The

2,832 participants were American men and women aged forty-five to seventy-seven who had no cardiac or other serious disease at the beginning of the study. The results were statistically adjusted for demographic and other risk factors of heart disease, so that these parameters would not influence the findings. (Because studies of quality are generally adjusted this way, we do not repeat this fact for each subsequent study. You can assume they have been adjusted, unless we say otherwise.)

Participants with depressed mood or hopelessness were one and a half to two times more likely to die from coronary artery disease than nondepressed participants. In addition, depression and hopelessness were associated with a higher incidence of nonfatal cardiac events, and more severe hopelessness was linked to a greater cardiac risk.

In addition, the study found that a depressed mood and hopelessness were more frequent among women, African-Americans, people with a lower level of education, singles, smokers, and those who were physically inactive.

Major and Minor Depression

Many studies have indicated that the more severe the depression, the greater the danger to the heart. For example, at Johns Hopkins University, researchers found that while minor depression raised the likelihood of a heart attack two times, major depression raised the likelihood up to four and a half times.

In another Johns Hopkins study, researchers analyzed the outcome of more than two hundred heart attack survivors. At four months after hospital discharge, those with very mild depression were six to seven times more likely to die than those who had no signs of depression. Those with moderate depression were eight to ten times more likely to die.

Depression and Unstable Angina

Patients with unstable angina account for a substantial portion of hospital admissions for coronary care. Researchers at the University of

Montreal interviewed 430 patients hospitalized with unstable angina and found that depressed patients were almost five times more likely to have a heart attack or die of cardiac causes than nondepressed patients. They found that depression is frequent following an episode of unstable angina and is associated with an increased risk of major cardiac events during the following year.

Does Gender Affect Depression's Link to Heart Disease?

In evaluating the association between depression and heart disease, many researchers have debated whether there is a gender difference. Conflicting studies on men and women have shown that the association between depression and heart disease in women is more complex than in men. This should not be surprising, because we know that although depression is more prevalent in women, they are protected from heart disease prior to menopause.

In one study where researchers compared cardiac events between men and women among their 5,623 British participants, depressed men did not do well. Men diagnosed with depression were three times more likely to develop ischemic heart disease than nondepressed men. The study concluded that depression might be an independent risk factor for coronary artery disease in men but not in women. However, researchers at Ohio State University College of Medicine and Public Health made some different conclusions after analyzing data from a study of 5,007 women and 2,886 men who were free of coronary artery disease on entering the study. Both women and men were 1.7 times more likely to develop coronary artery disease if they had suffered depression, but while depressed men were more than twice as likely to die of cardiac causes, depressed women showed no increase in death rate.

Depression and the Elderly:
An Important Risk Factor

As we mentioned in Chapter 3, depression among the elderly is a prevalent problem that has only recently received attention. When compared to elderly people without depressive symptoms, those with depression spend 50 percent more health-care dollars from more frequent use of medical services, a significant portion of which is for the diagnosis and treatment of heart disease.

Researchers focused on cardiovascular risk factors in the Cardiovascular Health Study, which involved Americans aged sixty-five and over, chosen at random from a county each in Maryland, North Carolina, Pennsylvania, and California. They set out to see whether depressive symptoms were related to coronary artery disease and death among the study's 4,493 participants who were free of cardiovascular disease at the beginning of the study, using data collected from 1989 to June 1996.

They reported that participants with the most severe depressive symptoms had a 40 percent greater risk of developing coronary artery disease and a 60 percent greater risk of death than those who had the fewest depressive symptoms.

In another study, researchers in Amsterdam, Holland, analyzed the association between depression and mortality among older community-dwelling people. Using data collected in a follow-up study of people aged fifty-five to eighty-five, drawn at random from eleven municipalities in three areas of Holland, a total of 3,056 men and women were followed up for four years. The results showed that both men and women with major depression had an almost twofold (1.83 times) higher risk of death than nondepressed men and women. (Interestingly, men with minor depression also had an almost twofold higher risk of death than nondepressed men. Women with minor depression did not have a significantly higher risk of death.)

These studies clearly emphasize the need for a high index of suspicion for depression in the elderly. If you're taking care of an elderly parent, for example, and you suspect he or she suffers from depression, a referral to a mental health professional should be strongly considered.

Depression as a Long-Term Risk Factor

Researchers at Johns Hopkins used data collected from 1,190 men in the Precursors Study of students who attended Johns Hopkins Medical School classes between 1948 and 1964 for their own study of long-term risks of depression and cardiovascular disease. During forty years of follow-up, 12 percent of the men developed major depression, but they had no differences in blood pressure, blood cholesterol level, smoking, physical activity, obesity, or family history of coronary artery disease. The depressed men were twice as likely to develop coronary artery disease and also twice as likely to have a heart attack. Ten years after their first episode of major depression, they were still twice as likely to have a heart attack as nondepressed participants.

While this lengthy duration of risk has been seen in many other studies, this one is particularly powerful because of its duration and the thoroughness of follow-up. It sends a clear message that depression, in the absence of other known risk factors, is associated with the development of coronary artery disease and a heart attack.

How Everyday Stresses Affect the Heart

Your body responds to external and internal stresses with physiological changes that help you deal with crises. This is called the *stress response*. After the stress passes, your body tries to return to its usual balance or equilibrium. You need to maintain your physiological state within a certain "normal" range. Living organisms have elegantly refined this process over millions of years. Humans need it to stay alive.

During each day, your body encounters innumerable physiological stimuli, to which it must respond appropriately. Scientists use the term *homeostasis* to describe the body's efforts to maintain a dynamically stable equilibrium. Another term, *allostasis*, refers to the maintenance of homeostasis. It literally means "to maintain stability or homeostasis through change." In allostasis, your physiological parameters are constantly being adjusted through brain mechanisms in order to adapt to internal and external environmental changes.

You don't notice these stimuli at all times, especially the minor ones. There is also no need for you to consciously make the adjustments necessary to meet these changes. With so much going on, virtually everything is on autopilot. When you rise in the morning, your blood pressure and heart rate have to increase in order to meet the greater blood flow demand. Climbing up a flight of stairs or going on a brisk walk requires more blood to the leg and heart muscles, a faster respiratory rate, and more glucose for fuel. When you get up from a chair, your blood pressure must be maintained to the brain or you will feel light-headed. During mealtimes, your blood needs to be redirected to your gastrointestinal system. At the end of the day, certain parts of your body slow down as you go to sleep. Because these are daily normal changes and take place countless times, we don't usually refer to them as stressors. The body responds to each of these changes in a precisely calibrated way—the allostatic response is seldom insufficient or inappropriate. These everyday stress responses are somewhat similar to the fight-or-flight response, except for their intensity, duration, and frequency.

But what do homeostasis, allostasis, and stress have to do with depression and coronary artery disease? When you are depressed, your body may be physiologically stimulated, a state that can damage your heart and circulatory system. In the following section, we look at how depression acts as a major stressor. At least some cases of depression are associated with an abnormality in the stress mechanism. While our discussion focuses on depression, some of the same principles are applicable to other negative emotions like anger and anxiety. We also speculate about how the body's stress responses can be damaging. We talk more about specific stress conspirators in Chapter 10.

How Depression Creates a Stress Response and Damages the Heart

The connection between the stress response and emotions such as anxiety and anger is easy to appreciate. For example, the physical manifestations of the stress response are the symptoms of anxiety. Rage, an extreme emotion, is a powerful stimulator of the sympathetic nervous system. However, looking at depression as a stressor is more difficult. After all, if someone has a depressed mood, sleeps many hours, feels tired, and expresses apathy toward things pleasurable, intuitively, it seems the individual's physical state should be just as depressed as the emotional state. Indeed, some theorists see depression as a brain by-product of an evolutionary adaptation to diseases such as infection and cancer. In this so-called sickness syndrome, it is proposed that the depressed individual is forced to conserve energy in a state of conservation-withdrawal.

Nevertheless, evidence points to depression as a major heart stressor. Numerous studies have documented evidence of sympathetic nervous system and cortisol hyperactivities during depression. The sympathetic and parasympathetic nervous systems make up the autonomic nervous system. Cortisol, known as the body's stress hormone, performs many critical functions that affect virtually every cell in the body. But it is not certain whether the increase in sympathetic nervous system and cortisol activities is a consequence or cause of depression.

Depression is associated with decreased heart rate variability, even in those without heart disease. Heart rate variability is a measure of heart healthiness. The brain regulates the heart via the autonomic nervous system, speeding up or slowing down the heart rate when appropriate. This suggests that cardiac disease and these negative mood states share autonomic dysfunction, leading to decreased heart rate variability. Whether this link reflects cause and effect, in one direction or another or in both directions, or is just associational (linked but of no consequence) remains to be seen.

Researchers at Emory University and others summed up four direct ways through which depression may cause coronary artery disease.

• *Overactivity of the hypothalamus-pituitary-adrenocortical (HPA) hormone system.* The HPA regulates the release of cortisol, a very important hormone for homeostasis and stress. Persistence of elevated cortisol levels has been associated with the insulin-resistance syndrome or metabolic syndrome, which in turn is thought to predispose to cardiovascular disease.

• *Imbalance of sympathetic and parasympathetic activation.* The autonomic nervous system includes sympathetic (mobilization) and parasympathetic (immobilization) components. This is another important system that the body uses to maintain homeostasis. The fight-or-flight stress response is included here.

• *Inadequate flow of blood to the heart muscle (myocardial ischemia) and ventricular irritability due to the stress response.*

• *Changes in blood platelet receptors or reactivity that make them stickier.* Platelets are blood components that initiate formation of a blood clot.

New data also suggest that depressive symptoms are associated with clotting on the basis of elevated levels of blood coagulation factors VII and X. There is also the possibility that heightened cell-mediated immunity with activated macrophages may play a role in both coronary artery disease and depression. We have already alluded, in Chapter 2, to the importance of macrophage-induced inflammation in coronary heart disease. Other researchers have proposed that macrophage activation also plays a role in depression.

Doctors at the National Institute of Mental Health have suggested that sustained activation of the two stress-response systems is involved in the long-term medical consequences of depression such as coronary artery disease. Research has not explained how exactly the systems are involved and is unlikely to do so for many years. At this point, what we are going to say should be considered speculative or hypothetical. However, our hypotheses are not without scientific basis.

One clinical finding that provides a valuable clue is the higher incidence of heart attacks during the early morning when there is a surge in the stress hormone cortisol level and a high state of sympathetic nerve arousal. As mentioned, there is a similar sympathetic and cortisol hyperactive state in depression. In such a state, blood vessels constrict and blood pressure becomes elevated, leading to high and turbulent blood flow. Two potential complications may result from this blood flow pattern. One potential complication is a localized injury to the vessel lining or intima, which then serves as a site where the process of atherosclerosis is initiated. Over many years in susceptible individuals, this injured intima gradually develops into coronary artery disease.

High, turbulent blood flow may also rupture a plaque, if preexisting coronary artery disease is already present. The ruptured plaque provides a surface for clot formation, resulting in a heart attack. This has been shown to be the mechanism for heart attacks in the early morning period.

Depression as a Risk Factor for Abnormal Blood Clot Formation

Clot formation in a coronary artery is a major contributor to heart attacks. Platelets in the blood are what initiate the process. When a blood vessel is cut, a complex process begins with the formation of a blood clot that eventually stops the bleeding. However, a blood clot can also form inside a vessel, usually in the setting of a damaged vessel lining or ruptured plaque. This clot can cut off blood flow and is one of the mechanisms in heart attacks. This is why aspirin and other antiplatelet agents are used to prevent or treat heart attacks.

Cortisol, epinephrine (also called adrenaline), and serotonin (a substance whose role in blood cells receives less popular attention than its role as a mood-enhancing neurotransmitter) have all been shown to alter the functions of blood platelets. A wealth of research has suggested that platelets in depressed people are particularly prone to activation. How do cortisol, epinephrine, and serotonin contribute to this abnormal platelet function? Cortisol is known to increase the stickiness of platelets and create a permissive environment where clots are more likely to form. In the setting of a damaged vessel lining or intima, a high cortisol level may encourage activation and clumping of blood platelets within a coronary artery, resulting in a heart attack.

Sympathetic activation is initiated in response to a variety of stimuli, which include tissue injury. Not surprisingly, sympathetic activation or, more specifically, epinephrine promotes platelet function and clot formation. While this nonspecific process is designed to stop bleeding in a cut vessel, it can also take place within a coronary artery, if the intima or a plaque is damaged. The end result may be a clot blocking blood flow and a heart attack.

Serotonin and its relation to depression have been studied intensely during the past few years. While the focus has been on the brain, platelets have also been investigated because they contain significant quantities of serotonin. Researchers showed that serotonin reuptake transporters are increased in the platelets of depressed people and suggested that this contributes to greater platelet activation. Selective serotonin reuptake inhibitor antidepressants appear to have antiplatelet activity as well.

Depression as a Risk Factor for Arrhythmias

A heart attack (myocardial infarction) is not the only potentially harmful consequence of depression. Malignant ventricular arrhythmia and sudden death are other candidates. In both of these conditions, the heart is more electrically irritable and susceptible to serious rhythm disturbances. How does depression increase cardiac arrhythmias?

Sympathetic hyperactivity associated with depression leads to a faster heart rate that in turn places the heart at risk for ventricular

Depression Mixed with Other Coronary Risk Factors

When a depressed person smokes, it may be more than an addiction to nicotine. Studies have found smoking to be more common among people who are depressed. This is very significant in that most of us know that smoking, among all the risk factors, has one of the strongest causal relationships to coronary artery disease. In a study of one hundred active smokers with a history of depression done at Columbia University, researchers noticed that a history of depression is more frequent among attendees at smoking-cessation classes, and people with a history of depression are more likely to resume smoking after a period of abstinence. They suggested that the emergence of major depression is a barrier to smoking cessation. They found that smokers who stopped smoking were seven times more likely to develop depression if they had a history of depression and were not on an antidepressant during smoking cessation.

arrhythmias, which are the usual causes of sudden cardiac death. The problem is more pronounced in a damaged heart, particularly within the scar tissues of a previous heart attack or in a heart with abnormal pump function. Rhythm disturbances can also result from a metabolic imbalance. A heart beating faster and harder requires more oxygen. In the presence of coronary artery disease, greater oxygen demand may not be met, and the ischemic regions of the heart are prone to arrhythmias.

Finally, both epinephrine and norepinephrine (also called noradrenaline) are potent agents that induce arrhythmias. On the other hand, brain serotonin may be a protective factor, because it is known to possess sympathetic inhibitory properties. A recent study showed that sertraline (Zoloft), a selective serotonin reuptake inhibitor (SSRI), facilitates recovery of cardiac autonomic function after a heart attack in patients with depression.

Depression and coronary artery disease—two dangerous disorders that affect millions of Americans—are linked in ways that have yet to be fully unraveled. Both disorders working together seem far more powerful than either one existing alone. It's also important to remember that the relationship between depression and coronary artery disease appears to travel in both directions. That is, coronary artery disease makes depression more likely while depression makes coronary artery disease more likely.

5

When Depression Comes After a Heart Attack

IF YOU OR SOMEONE you love has experienced a heart attack, you know that the possibility of mortality hits close to home. Everyone thinks about it, even though people rarely talk about it. For some fortunate patients, the heart attack is just a warning and there are no further physical consequences. For others, a heart attack signals the need for more testing, balloon angioplasty, or bypass surgery. For still others, it results in significant disability or death. In this chapter, we look at what happens when people suffer depression *after* they have survived a heart attack.

Understanding Your Cardiac Risk After a Heart Attack

A heart attack is both a physical and an emotional challenge. As a heart attack patient, you lose the veneer of invulnerability and develop a crisis of confidence. This is a normal reaction to a major illness. People usually have a high confidence level and a low vulnerability level, but a major illness tips the seesaw. It takes time and effort on the part of the patient, doctors, and support network to redress the imbalance.

What you may not have known until now is that depression is the best-kept secret after a heart attack, but it is not a benign complication: It slows down recovery, prolongs hospitalization, and increases the risk of another heart attack and death. Depression and the other heart-mind conspirators (discussed in Chapters 7 through 12) share responsibility in worsening high blood pressure, stroke, arrhythmias, and congestive heart failure, as well as coronary artery disease.

Risks of Cardiac Death: The First Six Months

Researchers at the Montreal Heart Institute and McGill University set out to determine whether major depression was an independent risk factor for cardiac mortality over the first six months after discharge from the hospital for a heart attack. They interviewed 222 patients (78 percent male) at a large, university-affiliated hospital in Montreal, who had all experienced a heart attack within the previous two weeks and who ranged in age from twenty-four to eighty-eight, with an average age of sixty. Those who had been diagnosed with major depression before discharge were more than four times at risk to die from cardiac causes within six months than those who were not.

These researchers concluded that major depression was not only a major risk factor for mortality but also as important as two other widely accepted independent risk factors: namely, a history of previous heart attacks and left ventricular dysfunction—when the heart is not pumping blood to the body as well as it normally does.

Affecting Recovery: Risk After Eighteen Months

The same researchers extended the study to eighteen months, and over this period, participants with major depression were about six and a half times more likely to die than the nondepressed. Those with major depression who also suffered ten or more premature ventricular contractions (abnormal heartbeats) per hour were twenty-nine times more likely to die. These findings led researchers to suggest that depression also promotes arrhythmia (irregular heartbeat) and sudden cardiac death. These same colleagues published a paper that went over some of the things they knew, didn't know, or weren't sure about. Among them were the following:

- Before a heart attack, people often suffer from a condition known as *vital exhaustion* (a combination of fatigue, irritability, and low morale).
- Depression immediately or even some time before a heart attack seems to negatively influence a patient's post–heart attack recovery.
- Patients who experience recurrent depressions have a more complicated recovery.
- Depression before a heart attack may influence how depression after a heart attack affects the patient's recovery.
- Those who become depressed after a heart attack frequently have experienced depression before the attack.
- During the first year after a heart attack, depression affects one in three people.

These studies implied that depression can potentially influence four very different but important processes:

- The development of an atherosclerotic plaque leading to coronary artery disease
- The rupture of a plaque and clot formation resulting in a heart attack
- Heart rhythm disturbances
- The psychological response to a major illness such as a heart attack

Furthermore, depression after a heart attack can further worsen the underlying heart disease, setting in motion a vicious cycle.

Cyclical Effect: Depression and Cardiac Rehabilitation

In an article from the Massachusetts General Hospital Cardiac Unit and Department of Psychiatry that included a review of the Montreal researchers' six- and eighteen-month follow-up studies of heart attack patients (which found depressed patients had increased risk of death

Some Dissenting Voices

There have also been some differences of opinion on the health risk associated with depression after a heart attack. Only 9 percent of patients had moderate to severe depressive symptoms after a heart attack in one study. Instead, symptoms of anxiety were prevalent. The reliability of this study has been questioned because of its design and other factors. For example, 12 percent of the screened patients were unable or unwilling to complete the questionnaire in the hospital, and the participants were overly represented by young men.

Another study found that neither depression nor anxiety predicted death from cardiac or other causes after a heart attack. The severity of the heart attack was the significant predictor of death among the study's participants. Depression and anxiety, however, greatly affected the quality of life of those who survived at least a year after their heart attack.

over six months, and even more over eighteen months), experts analyzed the influence of depression on people with established heart disease. The authors concluded the following:

- After a heart attack, 65 percent of people develop either major or minor depression.
- After a heart attack, 25 percent of people develop severe, often recurrent major depression.
- The Medical Outcomes Study showed that depression causes about as much disruption in daily functioning as does heart disease itself.
- The interaction of depression and advanced coronary artery disease causes almost twice the social impairment caused by either disorder alone.
- After a heart attack, depressed patients have more anxiety and stress than nondepressed patients.

Is It More than Depression? Other Psychological Cardiac Risk Factors

In a study of 222 heart attack patients published in *Health Psychology*, researchers found that the presence of major depression, depressive symptoms (minor depression), anxiety, or a history of major depression significantly predicted further cardiac events after recovery from a heart attack. Each had an impact independent of the others, and their impact was also independent of the severity of the original heart attack. These cardiac events included unstable angina, another heart attack, and arrhythmia.

These researchers emphasized that post–heart attack depression is not the only psychological factor affecting post–heart attack health. They particularly mentioned anxiety, inwardly directed anger, and depression previous to the heart attack. Interactions between negative emotions are enormously complex. Beyond that, each negative emotion affects cardiac health in various ways.

The Importance of Having a Positive Outlook During Recovery

In a study of 586 people aged thirty to fifty-nine, participants had no signs of heart disease themselves but had siblings who had heart problems at an early age. After physical and psychological tests, their health was followed over seven and a half years. Those participants whose psychological tests showed they had a positive outlook were only half as likely to experience heart problems as those with a negative outlook.

In another study, 160 people were evaluated for depression after suffering heart attacks. And 20 percent of the patients were found to be depressed. After four months, researchers checked to see whether the patients had followed their doctors' recommendations to change their lifestyles to improve their health. Some depressed patients were so convinced they would never get better, they refused to take steps that would have assisted their recovery. The worse they considered their health to be, the less likely they were to do anything about it. This same group was found to have a higher incidence of diabetes and high blood pressure.

The Influence of Social Support in Reducing Risk

Because depression interferes with the recovery process after a heart attack, whatever alleviates depression ought to assist in recovery. Responding to reports that social support lessens depression in cardiac patients, researchers looked into how social support helps people recovering from a heart attack. (By *social support*, they meant regular contact with a spouse or companion, close relative, and close friends.) They tested 887 patients for depression about a week after each had suffered a heart attack and followed the progress of each patient for a year.

Among those who had been depressed at the start of the study, high levels of social support helped reduce their depressive symptoms. Very high levels of social support saved the lives of patients indirectly by reducing their levels of depression, revealing that the more social support given to depressed patients, the lower their cardiac death rate.

A Treatment Strategy After Suffering from a Heart Attack

Twenty years ago, Drs. Thomas Hackett and Ned Cassem, specialists in cardiac psychiatry, developed a valuable treatment strategy for heart patients. We have adopted this five-part strategy throughout this book, because we think it is important, know it works, and use it in our clinical practices. If you or a loved one has suffered a heart attack, be sure to look at the following treatment strategy.

• Gather information from your doctor on both the typical and distinctive features of your condition, as well as insight into potential complications. The information should emphasize eventual success and be realistic. In this book, we pay special attention to dispelling myths and misinformation. You may have to gather some of this information on your own, from the Internet for instance, but if you do you should review it for accuracy with your doctor. In the Resources section, we provide some valuable Internet sources.

• Work with your cardiologist to begin appropriate activity, physical conditioning, and proper nutrition. We recommend cardiac rehabilitation (discussed further in Chapter 13) and encourage the patients to sign up.

• Anticipate certain frequent emotional stressors after a heart attack, such as depression, anxiety, and fear of being alone; develop a game plan for dealing with these situations.

• Consult with a psychiatrist to evaluate and manage conditions such as anxiety and depression. Treatment may include observation, supportive psychotherapy, or medications (discussed further in Chapter 14), depending on the severity.

• Consider behavioral therapies such as relaxation techniques for anxiety or cognitive behavioral therapy for depression. These approaches provide you with a sense of self-control over the stress of your illness. We provide some information on these behavioral therapies in Chapters 14 and 15.

Now that you are aware of the risks of depression after heart attack, you can look at the next chapter where we provide important information on the danger of depression before and after bypass surgery.

6

Depression Before and After Bypass Surgery

Peter had been married for more than forty years and had three children and four grandchildren. At age sixty-nine and retired from marketing, he led an active life. He played golf once a week, walked to local stores every morning, collected several of his grandchildren at their schools every afternoon, and then brought them to after-school activities and watched them until their parents returned from work.

Peter began to have chest discomfort from time to time, especially when he walked briskly. His family physician diagnosed the discomfort as angina caused by coronary artery disease, and he prescribed medications. When the angina persisted and perhaps even worsened slightly, the doctor referred Peter to a heart specialist. Additional testing confirmed the diagnosis of coronary artery disease. Blockages were found in several important coronary arteries, and after two unsuccessful attempts were made to reopen the arteries by balloon angioplasty, the heart specialist recommended bypass surgery. Its benefits and risks were explained to Peter and his wife. They were encouraged to ask questions. No one tried to hurry them into a decision. Later, however, neither Peter nor his wife remembered anyone even mentioning depression as a postoperative possibility. Peter signed the operative consent form, giving the surgical team permission to proceed with surgery.

On the day of surgery, Peter hadn't had a restful night; he had been thinking about what he would be facing the next morning. In the preanesthesia area, Peter removed his clothing and put on a skimpy hospital gown. When they took away his clothes, wallet, and other personal items, he felt he was losing his identity. He realized that things had to be done this way, but he wished he wasn't left feeling so physically and emotionally naked. The hospital staff members were polite and helpful, but there were so many of them and he felt confused and disoriented. Peter needed a quadruple bypass. After the surgery, he was moved to the intensive care unit where he remained overnight and was transferred to a regular room the next day. He was home within seven days of his surgery.

Six weeks after his surgery, Peter and his wife returned to the surgeon's office for a routine postoperative visit. His incision had healed nicely, and from the doctor's viewpoint, he seemed to be doing very well. His wife, however, took the doctor aside and mentioned some changes she had noticed. Prior to surgery, Peter had led an active life—he hadn't even allowed his angina to interfere with his activities. But after surgery, he hadn't taken up golf again. He never ran errands in the morning anymore. Most important, he seemed to have lost all interest in his grandchildren. He used to look forward to seeing them after school. Now he took a nap instead of collecting them.

WHILE IT IS TRUE that people who have been suffering from heart disease often emerge from cardiac surgery with better health, increased energy, and more optimism, there are known complications of bypass surgery. Depression is more common than any one of the better-known complications, yet it is seldom discussed with the patient. If you are scheduled for cardiac surgery, be sure that you discuss its "emotional" consequences—as well as potential physical consequences such as bleeding, infection, stroke, delirium, and death—with your doctor and your family.

Most people are aware of the risk of death from a coronary artery bypass operation. You might not wake up from the anesthesia. Or you might be unable to come off the breathing machine. Although these possibilities are frightening, the chances of their happening are very low. Many people know about other complications, such as bleeding, wound infection, pneumonia, heartbeat disturbances, and strokes.

These frightening, but not often deadly, complications are usually explained in detail to patients.

But depression as a complication after bypass surgery? This is virtually unknown to patients going for coronary bypass surgery, and it is almost never mentioned as a potential complication. Patients must realize that emotional difficulty, especially depression, is one of the most frequent complications of bypass surgery.

What Can Happen After Bypass Surgery

Most bypass patients end up with successful results—physically, that is. Their doctors say they are doing great, but they or their families notice something is not right—that they are not the same since surgery. Things that they once enjoyed no longer interest them. They may spend so many daylight hours asleep, they have trouble sleeping at night. Their appetite may be poor. Spousal relationships often deteriorate. Some are withdrawn, and others are irritable. Few have much of a sex drive. They may have trouble with remembering things, following directions, or doing simple calculations. In sum, patient improvement in physical health is sometimes matched by the deterioration in quality of life and at least temporarily in mental functioning.

Many people don't bring these complaints to the attention of their physicians. Some are embarrassed by the topic; others are not aware that a medical problem is involved and that it is treatable. Misconceptions are frequent. Some think that it is something that will pass. A few think that if they try harder, it will go away. Others don't want to bother their doctors with these "frivolous" complaints. They are afraid of appearing ungrateful. After all, the doctors saved their lives. Some patients who do discuss their complaints find that their doctors' responses are less than helpful.

Depression: Temporary and Longer Lasting

The attitude of many doctors has been that any depression or anxiety after a bypass is temporary and will fade away after the patient is discharged from the hospital. However, for the most part, research does not support this attitude.

In England, a research team looked for hard facts about how many bypass patients become depressed, and for how long. They studied 121 patients undergoing routine elective bypasses, testing them for depression four times—once before surgery and again at eight days, eight weeks, and twelve months after surgery. Their results were as follows:

- Thirty-seven percent of patients were depressed before surgery.
- Fifty percent of patients were depressed eight days after surgery.
- Twenty-four percent of patients were depressed eight weeks after surgery.
- Twenty-three percent of patients were depressed twelve months after surgery.

The presence of a major illness like heart disease and the prospect of open-heart surgery could easily explain the preoperative depression. The trauma of surgery and of being away from family, friends, and the familiarity of home could explain the early postoperative depression.

What's most surprising, though, is the finding that almost a quarter of the patients were still depressed at one year after surgery, suggesting that many patients are unable to fully enjoy all the benefits of this major operation. People can't take pleasure in the greater physical activities made possible by coronary bypass surgery if they are burdened with major depression. Of equal concern is the physical danger of depression, given what the medical profession now knows about the negative health effects of depression on the heart.

These researchers also made note that people with major depression before bypass surgery had a greater likelihood of being depressed after surgery. The study confirms the importance of identifying those patients who are depressed before and after surgery, because they would likely benefit from additional support. In addition, contrary to expectations, patients who needed fewer grafts (for example, single-bypass surgery) were more likely to be depressed after surgery than those who needed more grafts (for example, quadruple-bypass surgery). The researchers suggested that patients needing fewer grafts might have underestimated the physical impact of the invasive surgery. On the other hand, those needing more grafts may have been in worse physical shape before surgery and felt better after it. Being sicker, these patients may also feel more grateful that they have survived their surgery.

A team at Johns Hopkins University in Baltimore, Maryland, conducted a similar study using a different test for depression consisting of a twenty-question self-report questionnaire. They, like the researchers in England, also found a high incidence of depression before and after coronary bypass surgery. In addition, when they analyzed postoperative depression according to the absence or presence of preoperative depression, an interesting pattern emerged. For patients who were depressed before surgery, the incidence of postoperative depression among them was significantly higher at both one month and at one year than patients who were not depressed before surgery. These findings demonstrate that postoperative depression is linked to preoperative depression and that postoperative depression is not caused by the bypass operation alone.

Additional studies have shown a lower incidence of postoperative depression, while others have shown more frequent depression. Differences in the results of clinical studies are quite common. Even for the same coronary bypass operation, there are considerable differences in patient population among hospitals. Anesthetic techniques, surgical approaches, patient management, and methods used to assess depression can vary sufficiently to have an impact on the results.

Even with these differences, as a patient undergoing bypass surgery, keep in mind that depression after coronary bypass surgery is frequent, can persist for many months after the surgery, and is linked to a history of depression before surgery.

Brain Damage and Other Cerebral Complications

Most people who have bypass surgery are no longer young. The combination of advanced years and coronary artery disease increases their chances of postsurgical brain damage, such as stroke, or other cerebral complications, such as delirium, which develops over a short period of time, may fluctuate, and is comprised of a disturbance of consciousness, awareness, memory, orientation to time and place, perception, and language.

In fact, neurological complications are a significant cause of deaths after coronary bypass surgery, because bypass surgery itself exposes patients to circulatory system risks and the danger of stroke. Additionally, inflammation and immune reactions caused by surgery may contribute to nervous system damage and cerebral complications. We include these neurological complications because, as a patient, it is important for you to recognize that they are also major causes of post-operative depression.

In one of the more important studies that examined the cerebral complications of 2,108 bypass patients at twenty-four American hospitals, researchers found that type I complications (stroke, stupor, or coma at discharge) and type II complications (deterioration in intellectual function, memory deficit, or seizures) each occurred in 3 percent of the patients. While the incidence of type I was within the ballpark of most other reports, many heart specialists, including myself, dispute this rather low incidence of type II. The general consensus is that deterioration in intellectual function and memory deficits are common after coronary bypass surgery, especially after an episode of delirium. In the elderly, for instance, the incidence of delirium after cardiac surgery in one recent study was 23 percent.

Cognitive Decline

People quite frequently complain that their mental abilities, commonly referred to as *cognitive functions*, deteriorate after bypass surgery. But actual cognitive dysfunction can be much more subtle and may not be recognized as such by people it affects. After bypass surgery, you may likely complain that your memory is not as good as it was before surgery. Memory problems are the most important early cognitive impairment. You may also have problems with doing calculations, following directions, and playing complicated games such as chess. Manual dexterity may deteriorate. Concentration may worsen. To some patients, it may seem as if they have a mild form of Alzheimer's disease.

Cognitive dysfunction can be both short term and long term. Reported incidence of cognitive decline after coronary bypass surgery is quite variable, due to different tests being used and the sensitivity of each test. The incidence of short-term (less than one month after surgery) cognitive decline has ranged from 30 to 80 percent, while the

Table 6.1 Cognitive Decline After Bypass Surgery

Time After Bypass Surgery	Percentage of Patients with Cognitive Decline
Discharge from hospital	53 percent
Six weeks after surgery	36 percent
Six months after surgery	24 percent
Five years after surgery	42 percent

incidence of long-term (six months after surgery) decline is less, ranging from 20 to 50 percent.

A study at Duke University found incidences of cognitive decline among 261 patients after bypass surgery, as seen in Table 6.1. The study also found that late cognitive decline was linked to the severity of early cognitive impairment.

This report confirms that the prevalence of mental deterioration during the early period after bypass surgery is high. These findings should be taken seriously and warrant further investigation. Surgeons need to be cautious in telling patients that cognitive impairment is "temporary."

Strokes and Delirium

Stroke is a major complication of open-heart surgery. Fortunately, it is infrequent, occurring in 1 to 5 percent of patients after coronary bypass surgery. Patients who suffer from a stroke usually show weakness on one side of the body, and when the damage is in the dominant (usually the left) brain hemisphere, there can be language dysfunction called *aphasia*. Another serious manifestation of stroke can be coma. The symptoms of a stroke can be temporary or permanent or may partially improve with time. Strokes prolong hospitalization, result in other complications, and are associated with a high mortality. A major stroke frequently negates most of the benefits of coronary bypass surgery.

Another neurological complication, delirium, is more common than strokes after coronary bypass surgery. Described earlier, it is usually manifested by disorientation, agitation, perceptual changes and delusions, sleep-wake reversals, and cognitive deficits. Delirium usually reverses over several days. This complication occurs after bypass surgery in 10 to 30 percent of patients, according to a 2001 study. This condition is thought to be related to anesthesia and medications, reduced cerebral blood flow, or microemboli (microscopic particles that clog the small capillaries in the brain). Older patients and those with a heavy drinking history are particularly prone to develop delirium.

The Link Between Brain Damage and Depression

A patient waking up from his or her coronary bypass surgery paralyzed on one side from a stroke is at very high risk for major depression. Someone who is unable to concentrate or who realizes that his or her intellectual function has deteriorated after surgery will likely feel frustrated and, quite possibly, depressed. Researchers have noted that bypass patients who reported a decline in their cognitive function tended to be depressed and anxious. It is also recognized that depression can result in cognitive decline.

In a study done six weeks after bypass surgery, researchers at Duke University Medical Center found that the significant cognitive decline shown by 37 percent of the patients was strongly associated with depression and anxiety. However, they noted that test scores and patients' perception of their own cognitive decline often did not agree. This means that patients suffering from depression and anxiety were more likely to perceive a decline in their cognitive abilities that was not backed up by their tests scores. When they were treated for their emotional distress, their perceived cognitive decline was likely to lessen.

How Depression Affects Recovery

Recovery after bypass surgery can depend as much on a patient's emotional state as it does on the condition of the patient's heart. When researchers at the University of Maryland Medical Center in Baltimore looked at many factors—including age, gender, marital status, smoking behavior, and depression—in 309 bypass patients (207 men and 102 women), they found that only depression, heart condition, and gender mattered and that they were of equal importance.

Their study included the following findings:

- Patients depressed in the hospital were at least three times more likely to have a cardiac problem in the year following surgery than nondepressed patients.
- Women, regardless of emotional state, had a three times greater risk than men of further cardiac events.
- Almost half (47 percent) of depressed women suffered a cardiac event during the year following surgery, compared with 18 percent of nondepressed women.
- Cardiac events were suffered by 20 percent of depressed men during the year following surgery, compared with 6 percent of nondepressed men.

In another study showing the negative health consequence of depression on the heart, researchers in Stockholm, Sweden, had 171 consecutive bypass patients complete questionnaires before surgery and a year after surgery. The medical charts were followed up for three years, and researchers found that the surgical results were excellent in the majority of cases. However, patients with a high degree of preoperative distress (depression, anxiety, and fatigue) assessed their status as much worse both before surgery and at the one-year follow-up. At the three-year follow-up, 16 percent of emotionally distressed patients had suffered further cardiac events, in contrast to the 5 percent of nondistressed patients.

Higher Death Rate Among Depressed Patients

In a study of 158 Australian bypass patients, 24 were classified as depressed and 134 as not depressed. The postoperative mortality rate among the depressed was 12 percent, and among the nondepressed it was 2 percent. While the depressed group was small, this study suggests that depressed patients not only have a lesser quality of life but also are at a higher risk of dying after their coronary bypass surgery.

Higher Risk of Rehospitalization Among Depressed Patients

Psychologists at Carnegie Mellon University looked at patients in recovery and noticed that optimistic patients are less likely to be rehospitalized for problems related to their surgery or coronary artery disease than less optimistic patients (see Table 6.2).

However, the study points out that depression is a more reliable predictor of a patient's negative health outcome than optimism is of a positive outcome. Researchers also cautioned that optimism and pessimism should not be equated with nondepression and depression.

If You Are Having or Need Bypass Surgery

When going for bypass surgery, make sure you are screened for depression both pre-op and post-op, because depression is associated with poorer outcomes.

When there is a suspicion of depression or cognitive problems—and keep in mind that elderly patients are especially at risk—insist that a psychiatrist be consulted as early as possible so that you can receive help if you need it. Psychiatrists can assist cardiac surgeons by recommending appropriate tests and medications. They can explain situations to you and your family and suggest behavioral and supportive

Table 6.2 Risk of Hospitalization After Surgery

Type of Patient	Risk for Hospitalization
Optimistic patients	Less likely to be rehospitalized
Depressed patients	More likely to be rehospitalized and suffer wound infection
Neurotic patients (those who misinterpret events due to prior conditioning and experiences)	More likely to be rehospitalized
Low-self-esteem patients	More likely to be rehospitalized

therapies, some of which can be very simple. For example, a clock, calendar, and frequent reorientation, as well as plenty of family member visits, help patients who are disoriented. A soft nightlight may also be helpful. To have the best outcome, you need to be monitored for depression and given treatment, if necessary. We talk about treatment options in more detail in Part III of this book.

Once discharged from the hospital, your mental functioning will usually return to normal over the ensuing months. However, in some patients, cognitive decline will persist and possibly even worsen. If cognitive function slows down, you will need follow-up evaluations. This may reveal itself through difficulties concentrating, remembering what you have read, performing routine calculations (such as balancing a checkbook), and following directions. Memory-enhancing medications such as donepezil (Aricept) or memantine (Namenda) may eventually be warranted. Sometimes, treating depression with antidepressants (discussed further in Chapter 14) or cognitive behavior therapy carries the added bonus of improving cognition, because depression can worsen memory. Sleep problems need to be noted and treated.

Cardiac rehabilitation programs can be very helpful in increasing optimism and improving mood. Hospitals often have their own programs or refer patients to approved programs. Your surgeon, cardiologist, and family doctor can provide advice. Help for the caregiving spouse from such a program can also smooth your recovery. After surgery, you need to be encouraged to see old friends and meet new people. For many people, the comfort and solace that religion can provide is also helpful.

So far you have examined the various links between depression (the chief conspirator) and heart disease. However, there are seven other heart-mind conspirators that need to be explored for their risks and effects on heart disease, which we will now go into in the second part of our investigation of the heart-mind connection.

PART II

Examining the Other Heart-Mind Conspirators

7

Anxiety

Going to the Heart
of the Matter

Helen, who lived with her husband outside Milwaukee, underwent an uncomplicated quadruple-bypass surgery. Her postoperative course should have been equally uneventful. But four days after her surgery, she developed breathing difficulty. Tests revealed no physical cause for her shortness of breath. However, when the doctors were making bedside rounds one evening, her daughter said that Helen had had similar episodes during the past two years, for which she took antianxiety medication. Upon more detailed questioning, Helen said she had always been the nervous type. In recent years, she had developed shortness of breath, usually brought on by fears of dying and suffocation. She said she felt restless, warm, and sweaty with each occurrence. At these times she also often felt tired and had trouble sleeping.

Her doctors diagnosed her shortness of breath as anxiety. After reassurance and resuming her antianxiety medication, Helen's breathing difficulties improved.

CHEST PAIN AS A manifestation of anxiety is more common than people realize. It becomes tricky because a panic attack can often be mistaken for a heart attack. Patients may go from doctor to doctor because the cause of their chest pain is unclear. Is it a coronary artery spasm? Is it only psychosomatic? Or, is it both? We know that anxiety can be a consequence of heart disease, a heart attack, or surgery and that after open-heart surgery, there can be many causes of breathing difficulty (e.g., a partially collapsed lung, or atelectasis; a pulmonary embolus; pneumonia; heart failure; and fluids around the lungs, or pulmonary effusion). However, it is important to realize that anxiety is also a possible cause. If the anxiety is significant, it requires attention just like any other complication after surgery.

Everyone feels anxiety at some point, and anxiety is a natural response to dealing with a life-threatening illness like cardiac disease. But severe chronic anxiety, if left untreated, can also be a risk factor for heart attack and sudden death, which is why it is the focus of this chapter.

Anxiety: Depression's Frequent Companion

As a frequent sidekick of depression—the most powerful of the heart-mind conspirators and the subject of many research investigations—anxiety has been included in a number of research studies. However, there's been much less research into anxiety as an independent risk factor for coronary artery disease.

As with depression, researchers use a scale to measure a person's level of anxiety. The scale usually consists of a questionnaire with numeric values assigned to the answers. But an accurate diagnosis is further complicated in that there are more kinds of anxiety than there are varieties of depression. For diagnostic purposes, American psychiatrists divide anxiety into a number of anxiety disorders. You are described as having an emotional disorder when your condition interferes with your daily life, including your quality of life. So, theoretically, two people could have the same amount of anxiety and only one have an anxiety disorder. The person who can manage and thus reduce the effect of his or her anxiety so that it does not disrupt daily life does not have an active anxiety disorder.

You may notice that we use the word *manage* quite often when talking about stress and emotions like anxiety and anger. While stress and emotions may be almost impossible for you to avoid, you often can manage them. We also provide you with some ways to manage your anxiety in Chapter 15.

Types of Anxiety Disorders

Anxiety disorders are what used to be called *neuroses*. In much the same way that depressed mood and loss of interest are the most important symptoms of depression, those of anxiety disorders are *anxiety* (a feeling of pervasive worry, usually in the absence of an actual physical threat) and *avoidance behavior* (when you try to avoid the stressful thing or any reminder of it).

In addition, each type of anxiety disorder has unique features that doctors use to make the diagnosis. Not all psychiatrists agree about dividing anxiety into these disorders and/or they have reservations about them. Nevertheless, at present, the consensus is to characterize anxiety disorder into the following subgroups:

- Generalized anxiety disorder
- Post-traumatic stress disorder
- Obsessive-compulsive disorder
- Simple phobia
- Social phobia
- Agoraphobia
- Panic disorder

Generalized Anxiety Disorder

Anxiety, an excessive or unrealistic worry that something bad is going to happen, is a feeling familiar to most of us. Parents tend to worry about their children; career-driven individuals about business; and high school and college kids about their popularity, exams, or sports. There's no end of things to worry about at all stages in your life. But when you have this fear about two or more events or activities for six months or longer, and have the following physical symptoms, you may have a generalized anxiety disorder. For the diagnosis to be made, in addition to this excessive anxiety, three or more of the following symptoms must be present:

- Restlessness or feeling on edge
- Fatigue
- Problems concentrating or mind going blank

- Irritability
- Muscle tension
- Trembling
- Shortness of breath

People with this disorder frequently also suffer from minor depression (which we discussed in Chapter 3) and are at risk for major depression, and many people with generalized anxiety disorder will tell you that they are worriers who have felt nervous all their lives.

If you are experiencing these symptoms, check with your doctor to obtain a definitive diagnosis, because all of these symptoms can also be the side effects of a general medical condition or of a chemical. Many medical conditions, such as thyroid disease, chronic obstructive lung disease, and adrenal hyperactivity, can cause you to have symptoms of anxiety. Caffeine in coffee, tea, and soda can also cause you to develop anxiety symptoms. Some over-the-counter medications, such as cold preparations and diet pills, contain agents that are stimulants. You should also be cautious about herbal products that may contain stimulants; ginseng is one in particular.

Post-Traumatic Stress Disorder

People who have witnessed a highly distressing event can repeatedly reexperience it and suffer symptoms because of this. To qualify for post-traumatic stress disorder, the event has to be out of the ordinary, such as a serious threat or actual harm to yourself or others close to you, someone's injury or violent death, or destruction of your home or community. (Normal mourning over the loss of a loved one, marital problems, long-term illness, or financial losses, while painful, don't count.) The stress felt by Vietnam War veterans long after that conflict first made post-traumatic stress widely known, and we now know that many others who were involved in the tragedies of September 11, 2001, have begun to suffer from the disorder. Some people who undergo open-heart surgery or suffer a life-threatening heart ailment afterward develop symptoms typically seen in post-traumatic stress.

With post-traumatic stress disorder, you may reexperience the traumatic event as a flashback, nightmare, recollection, or symbol (for example, on its anniversary). You may try to avoid anything that reminds you of the event or, alternatively, you may deaden yourself to anything associated with it. Reexperiencing the event may cause you to suffer the following physical symptoms:

- Sleeplessness
- Irritability or anger
- Extreme watchfulness
- Problems in concentrating
- Fearful sweating

Obsessive-Compulsive Disorder

Obsessions are recurrent thoughts. Compulsions are repetitive actions. When persistent thoughts and actions interfere with your daily life, you may have obsessive-compulsive disorder. You realize, at least at the beginning, that your obsessions are senseless and intrusive and that they are a product of your mind (that is, you're not hearing voices). The most frequent obsessions are about acts of violence, fears of contamination, and doubts about whether you have or have not done something. For example, people with an obsession about cleanliness may have a compulsion to wash their hands very frequently. The private detective lead character of the television series "Monk" is portrayed as someone who is amusingly self-aware of his obsessions but unable to control his compulsions.

With this disorder, your compulsions are acts or behaviors that ease the distress that your obsessions are causing you. Your acts are usually repetitive, but you know what you're doing and that your behavior may strike others as eccentric. Yet you get a release of tension by doing these things, so when you try to resist your compulsions, tension builds.

Simple Phobia

A simple phobia is a persistent fear of something. Most simple phobias are of animals, especially snakes, mice, and insects. Fear of heights, closed spaces, blood, and air travel are others. Your anticipation or endurance causes you to have anxiety symptoms—such as trembling or shortness of breath—although you realize that your fear is excessive or unreasonable.

However, simple phobia does not rank as a disorder until your avoidance or endurance of the thing feared disrupts your daily life. For example, if you have a fear of heights and have had to turn down a desirable job because it entailed working on the eighth floor of a building, your phobia has interfered with your daily life and qualifies as a disorder. On the other hand, fear of something rarely encountered in your environment is less likely to qualify as a disorder, unless that fear forces you to remain in such an environment.

Social Phobia

With social phobia, your fear of embarrassing or humiliating yourself in public causes you symptoms of anxiety, such as feelings of panic, rapid heartbeat, or sweating. Your fear can be about an array of things, including public speaking, not being able to answer questions, or eating in restaurants. Frequently, this fear is based on an actual incident in which you felt embarrassed or humiliated, and the possibility of the same or a similar incident occurring again arouses feelings of apprehension. If you try to ignore your phobia and deliberately place yourself in circumstances in which the feared thing can readily occur, your level of anxiety may rise to an intolerable level unless there are strategies in place to reduce it.

Agoraphobia

Agoraphobia is the fear of being someplace where you can't escape easily or without embarrassment or where you can't get help easily if something happens to you. You often have a specific situation in mind. For example, one person may fear developing cardiac distress among uncaring strangers and being left unaided. Another may fear losing bladder or bowel control and being unable to find a bathroom. Still another person may fear becoming dizzy, falling down, and being left lying on a street. To avoid the anxiety caused by such situations, you restrict your activities or take a companion along. In some rare cases, people do not leave their houses or apartments.

Panic Disorder

Panic attacks are like phobias, but they occur without warning and in the absence of any obvious cause. With experience, however, you may recognize the circumstances under which you are most likely to be affected. Medically, the condition of panic disorder is usually diagnosed if you experience either of the following:

- You have four panic attacks over the course of four weeks.
- You spend four weeks dreading another panic attack after suffering one.

Your panic disorder may also be accompanied by the previously discussed agoraphobia.

The anxiety symptoms of panic attacks are noted for their intensity and unpleasantness. In other words, the symptoms are much the same as those of anxiety—muscle tension, shortness of breath, palpitations and chest discomfort, thoughts of impending doom, and so on—but the level of discomfort and acuteness of distress these symptoms cause is likely to be much greater. In addition, you may have vivid flashbacks and recurrent nightmares about disturbing incidents in the past. Because of the unpredictability and intensity of the symptoms, psychiatrists regard panic attacks as a more serious threat than other forms of anxiety.

In this chapter, panic attacks are considered under the heading of anxiety. But panic attacks also rank as an independent heart-mind conspirator because of their potential association with heart attack, including chest pain and shortness of breath. You can find more about chest pain and panic disorder in Chapter 11.

The Link Between Anxiety Disorders and Sudden Cardiac Death

All of us have heard of someone suddenly "dropping dead." There are many causes for sudden death, but the heart is a major one. In most cases of sudden cardiac death, the cause is a very rapid, ineffective beating of the ventricles; doctors call this *malignant ventricular arrhythmia*. In this condition, the heart beats so rapidly and ineffectively that no blood is being pumped out of the heart, and death follows in a matter of minutes. This is the reason why ambulances, airplanes, and many public facilities now carry a defibrillator to electrically shock the heart back into a regular rhythm. Malignant ventricular arrhythmia has several causes:

- Myocardial infarction (lack of oxygen resulting in blocked blood flow to the heart)
- Spasm of the coronary artery
- A surge in adrenaline, especially in people prone to coronary artery spasm or who have coronary artery disease

Although it has long been known that psychiatric patients with anxiety disorders have a high death rate, only recently have studies linked anxiety to the development of heart trouble in the general population. In three community-based studies, researchers established links between anxiety disorders and cardiac death. The only drawback to these studies is that even though anxiety disorders are more frequent among women than men, the studies didn't include any women. Still, researchers discovered the following:

- Men with the highest levels of phobic anxiety were almost four times more likely to die from coronary artery disease than men with no anxiety.
- The most anxious men in this study were two and a half times more likely to die from coronary artery disease than the least anxious.
- Men with nonphobic symptoms of anxiety in this study were more than four times as likely to die from coronary artery disease.

The deaths attributed to anxiety in these three studies were not from heart attacks but from sudden cardiac death. This caused the researchers to suggest that malignant ventricular arrhythmias may have been the cause of death. People with anxiety disorders tend to have less variability of their heart rate, an indication of an underlying heart problem. Indeed, the problem could involve increased stimulation of the sympathetic nervous system.

Researchers have also found links between panic disorder and coronary artery disease and between worry and coronary artery disease. Other smaller studies have shown links between anxiety and an array of cardiac events, including heart attacks.

The Link Between Anxiety Disorders and Heart Attack

Almost half the people admitted to hospital coronary care units suffer from anxiety. Most of them are undiagnosed and untreated for this emotional condition. Researchers who reviewed a number of studies linking anxiety to poor outcome and death in people with known coronary artery disease found the following disturbing facts:

- People with anxiety after a heart attack are two and a half times more likely to have additional cardiac complications.
- Survivors of a heart attack who have a high level of anxiety while still in the hospital have a fivefold increase in risk of more coronary artery disease problems, another heart attack, and death. In addition, anxiety following a heart attack is one of the most reliable predictors of in-hospital complications.

Researchers reviewing these studies suggested that an exaggerated sensitivity to stress causes some of the anxiety that affects the heart. In addition, there are the additive effects of behavioral risk factors that anxious people are prone to, such as smoking and excessive coffee drinking. Although we can never be certain whether anxiety actually contributes to a second heart attack and death, we now know from a number of studies that anxiety can have a negative health consequence on the heart and therefore should not be taken lightly.

In addition, some survivors of heart attacks are so overwhelmed by the experience that they develop post-traumatic stress disorder as a result. Patients who have been in an intensive care unit (ICU), particularly a respiratory ICU, are among the most likely to develop post-traumatic stress disorder.

Researchers at Mount Sinai Medical Center in New York City followed 102 patients for six months to a year after they suffered a heart attack. Of the patients, 40 percent had the avoidance symptoms characteristic of post-traumatic stress disorder. In other words, these patients went out of their way to try to avoid any reminders of their stressful heart attacks. About 10 percent had the intrusion symptoms of post-traumatic stress disorder, including flashbacks and nightmares. Another 10 percent had both avoidance and intrusion symptoms.

All were less likely to be compliant with their medications than similar patients without post-traumatic stress disorder. This compliance problem was greater among the 10 percent who had both avoidance and intrusion symptoms. For this reason, if you or someone you know is reliving the experience of a heart attack or of bypass surgery, talk to the physician right away, because of the higher cardiac risk involved with anxiety conditions like post-traumatic stress disorder.

Treating the Anxious Heart

In the acute setting, especially in the coronary care unit, anxiety is usually managed with antianxiety medications such as benzodiazepines—for example, lorazepam (Ativan), oxazepam (Serax), alprazolam (Xanax)—and the non-benzodiazepine buspirone (BuSpar). Benzodiazepines are usually more helpful than buspirone in the acute setting, because buspirone can take two to three weeks to take effect. Relaxation techniques and supportive therapy are often helpful, as is the encouragement of a strong social support network, including spiritual sources of support. We talk about these treatment options in greater detail in Part III of this book.

In general, your acute adjustment reactions should not last for more than six months after the end of the acute event or stressor. In more chronic adjustment disorders, your symptoms may persist for six months or longer. This can occur when your medical illness is of long duration or your acute medical illness results in long-term complications. Coronary artery disease can fit this profile.

Anxiety, and for that matter, depression, may be considered perfectly normal reactions to a heart attack or coronary bypass surgery, especially close to the time of these events. Nevertheless, if the mood change causes marked distress out of proportion to what is expected or if there is significant psychosocial impairment, the condition may be considered an adjustment disorder with anxious or depressed mood and should be treated. Vigilance about developing major depression is required.

If you have suffered a cardiac event and develop any of the anxiety disorders described in this chapter, you can get specific psychiatric treatments for all these disorders. For example, selective serotonin reuptake inhibitors (SSRIs)—discussed in Chapter 14—can be effective against obsessive-compulsive disorder, post-traumatic stress disorder, social phobia, and panic disorder. Cognitive behavioral therapy has also been shown to be very helpful in the treatment of anxiety disorders.

Healthy habits can also reduce the levels of stress that exacerbate anxiety states. Relaxation exercises, lifestyle and behavior changes, exercise, good nutrition, social supports, and spiritual practices (which are all covered in Chapter 15) can help. Ideally, you don't want to wait until you have developed heart disease or anxiety disorder to cultivate these healthy habits. It's never too early—or too late—to begin a healthy lifestyle.

8

Anger

The Most Damaging Component of a Type A Personality

Twelve patients with known coronary artery disease were studied as they underwent coronary catheterization (a diagnostic test to determine the amount of blockage in the coronary arteries). The researchers asked the patients to recall a recent event that had produced anger. The simple memory of anger caused constrictions of sclerotic (plaque-containing) coronary arteries but not healthy ones. However, the constriction occurred only with high levels of anger. While it was a small study, the findings showed that constriction or spasm in an atherosclerotic coronary artery precipitated by anger may result in angina or even a heart attack.

MANY PEOPLE BELIEVE that having a type A personality (that is, having traits that are predominately hostile, competitive, impatient, aggressive, and controlling) is a risk factor for heart disease, but only one component of this personality clearly poses a threat to the heart. Recent studies have found anger to be the significant risk factor. Twenty years ago, someone with a hard-driving type A personality was seen as a prime candidate for coronary artery disease and a heart attack. Today, we understand that any type of personality is likely to have a heart attack if a person is more likely to express anger in inappropriate ways.

Type A Behavior and Hostile Expressions of Anger

Most people know someone (or perhaps are that someone!) who fits this description: is impatient, frequently displays a sense of urgency, speaks loudly and explosively, is competitive, and is excessively dedicated to work. This person has classic type A behavior. In 1981, a National Institutes of Health review panel found an association between type A behavior and the development of coronary artery disease. Despite early supportive findings in these studies, later research failed to support this association.

So researchers looked more closely at type A behavior itself. What if some components of type A behavior were harmless and others were tied to cardiac risk? A number of studies (such as the one that introduced this chapter) led to hostility being selected as the toxic component. These researchers regarded hostility as a personality trait. In a review of studies, hostility was seen to be made up of three components:

1. A prevailing attitude of cynical mistrust toward others
2. A propensity toward anger
3. A tendency to express anger by arguing, speaking loudly, and/or physical assault

Cynical mistrust is quite different from anger. It consists of holding misanthropic beliefs, including the universal attribution of selfish motives to other people's acts. Anger, on the other hand, consists of an emotional state that can range from mild irritation to annoyance to rage and fury, usually in response to perceived provocation or mistreatment. Of the three components of hostility, the third—the expression of anger through arguing, speaking loudly, and/or physical assault—is the only one that has been significantly linked to coronary artery disease.

Linking Anger and Coronary Risk

In a study of 1,305 men with a mean age of sixty-one years who were free of coronary artery disease at the beginning, high levels of anger were studied and were found to increase the risk of coronary artery disease. Subjects completed a test that measured the degree to which they had problems controlling their anger. Researchers followed up the health of the subjects for an average of seven years. The researchers found that anger in these men caused a two- to threefold increase in the risk of angina pectoris (acute chest pain due to decreased blood supply to the heart) and coronary artery disease. This report substantiated other studies that found anger could precipitate a heart attack.

Researchers also found that aspirin reduced the effects of anger on coronary artery disease risk; regular users of aspirin had approximately half the risk of nonusers.

Linking Anger and Heart Attacks

People who have frequent episodes of anger have repeated quickening of the heartbeat and raising of the blood pressure. In conjunction with coronary constriction, this excessive reactivity might promote rupture of the atherosclerotic plaque in the coronary artery and lead to the formation of a blood clot. As you may recall from Chapter 2, this is the process that precedes a heart attack. Beta-blockers may reduce the blood pressure response that leads to plaque disruption, while aspirin may decrease the platelet aggregation and reduce the likelihood of clot formation.

In one study, researchers interviewed 1,623 people (about a third of them women) usually four days after they had suffered a heart attack. Interviewers asked them about place, time, and pain intensity of the heart attack as well as the frequency of their anger during the previous year. They also inquired about the time and intensity of any anger felt during the twenty-four hours prior to the heart attack.

In the two hours after an anger outburst, those who were not regular users of aspirin were found to have had a threefold increased risk of a heart attack. Regular users of aspirin had half this increased risk in the two hours after an anger outburst. Users of beta-blockers also had a lower risk but this finding did not reach a significant threshold.

Combining Anger with Other Risk Factors

Risk factors seldom act alone. They tend to interact with one another and increase risks; as discussed in earlier chapters, combinations of risk factors can be more powerful than single risk factors alone. Combination of emotional and behavioral risk factors takes place all the time. For example, when people are angry, they may smoke and drink more. In any one person, however, it's often not clear to what extent anger is an independent risk factor and to what extent it is operating in conjunction with other risk factors.

A dangerous combination of risk factors involves anger, lower socioeconomic status, and an unhealthy lifestyle. Economically disadvantaged people given to outbursts of anger who drink a lot, smoke, and don't have family or close friends fit this profile. Level of education counts, too, because less-educated people are more likely to be unaware of the health risks of some of their acts and to have less access to healthy behavioral outlets for their negative moods.

Anger and Low Social Support with Coronary Artery Disease

A combination of high hostility and low social support (discussed further in Chapter 9) is known to increase your risk of coronary artery disease and death from cardiac causes. In one study that set out to measure the direct effect on coronary arteries of such a combination of high hostility and low social support—independent of the effects of adverse health—researchers credited emotional support as the component of social support that had the strongest influence on coronary artery disease. In the trial, 223 people with known coronary artery disease had an arteriogram to document the location and severity of the blockages in the coronary arteries. They answered three questionnaires, and after two years, 162 of them had a second arteriogram. The arteriograms were analyzed by expert cardiologists who had no detailed knowledge of the trial. Through a follow-up on the health of the trial participants, researchers found that those with low social support who expressed anger outwardly had a more than threefold increased risk of progression of their already existing coronary artery disease.

Depression and Hostility After a Heart Attack

Depression and hostility frequently coexist in people getting medical attention. They also share similar biochemical profiles—that is, they affect the body physiologically along similar pathways. Dr. Fricchione, one of the coauthors, took part in a study with M. W. Kaufmann and others to find the relationships among depression, hostility, heart attacks, and death. The participants of the study were all in the hospital after a heart attack and consisted of 217 men and 114 women, with a mean age of sixty-five years. A total of three hundred were diagnosed with cynical hostility, and ninety with major depression. Of the ninety with major depression, eighty-four also tested positive for cynical hostility—a remarkable overlap of depression and hostility in post–heart attack patients.

Some researchers refer to patients with cynical hostility and depression as *type D* or *distress personality*. Others regard what they call negative affectivity as a basic personality trait that increases the tendency for individuals to experience negative emotions.

In a study of eighty-seven post–heart attack patients aged forty-one to sixty-nine, researchers found that emotional stress played a role in the outcome, regardless of the severity of the cardiac disorder. Type D patients had a 4.7 times greater risk of further cardiac events than non–type D patients.

Treating Angry Outbursts Before They Put You at Risk

If you find yourself having frequent angry outbursts, ask your doctor about taking an aspirin every day. It might make all the difference to your heart. Regular aspirin users are only half as likely as nonusers to pay cardiac consequences for their anger outbursts. It's also equally important to alter the way you respond to anger. Anger-management classes may be a good place to start, but you should also look for relaxation techniques (which we talk about more in Chapter 15), behavioral exercises, and training in interpersonal skill building.

Studies have pointed out that some people with depression are prone to sudden intense spells of anger that typically occur in situations in which the person feels emotionally trapped. These anger outbursts, described as being inappropriate to the conditions at hand, can be quite common. However, the good news is that treatment with selective serotonin reuptake inhibitors like sertraline and fluoxetine (discussed more in Chapter 14) is very effective. Fifty to seventy percent of depressed individuals with these attacks reported disappearance of their anger outbursts with treatment. We suggest treatment with an SSRI agent for depressed patients who are troubled with anger outbursts, as in this setting, SSRIs are likely to improve both their depression and their anger.

9

Social Isolation

No Man (or Woman) Is an Island

Dan was a stockbroker with a big financial services firm in midtown Manhattan. He was in his late thirties and had already been divorced twice. He had a steady girlfriend who was a stockbroker, too, and worked the same long hours he did, but for a rival firm. She understood how the market can take over people's minds and lives during busy times. She and Dan hung out together when they had the time and energy to do so, but this wasn't often. Dan knew people all over the world. At least, he knew their stock portfolios, which for him was like looking into the deepest recesses of their minds. On his computer, he had their car phone numbers; home e-mail addresses; dates of birth; and the names of spouses, children, and even pets. These were people he felt he really knew. Of course, he would have passed most of them in the street without recognizing them, because he had never actually met them. But he seemed to know thousands of people.

Josie, on the other hand, was about the same age as Dan and had a sweet nature but few social skills. She had dropped out of high school to care for her ailing mother, and they lived together in an apartment in Brooklyn until her mom died. Josie came into Manhattan on the subway every weekday to clean apartments. She had her own client list, charged what she felt was fair, and was choosy about who she worked for. She worked hard and was fastidiously honest. Her clients sometimes joked among themselves about why she charged some of them more than others. None knew why and dared not ask for fear of offending her. Josie was known to drop clients for no stated reasons. Her simple lifestyle, getting paid in cash, and living in a rent-controlled apartment allowed her to lead an independent life. She sang in a choir and had a network of friends, most of whom she had gone to school with, who lived in her Brooklyn neighborhood. Josie was godmother to their children, remembered people's birthdays, and visited everyone when they were sick.

Dan was recommended to Josie as a client. He left the keys for her with the doorman, and she went to inspect the apartment. All the blinds were drawn and lights had been left on, although it was bright daylight outside. There were stacks of papers everywhere—on the floor, the couch, tables, and chairs—each with a little yellow sticker on top that read: DO NOT TOUCH. A pile of newspapers more than three feet high was also not to be touched. The kitchen hadn't been used in ages—she could tell by the coating of dust on everything. She looked into the bedroom. It was a mess, but she didn't mind that. A second bedroom was empty except for computer equipment and boxes of files. Josie decided she could never clean an apartment like this. This man didn't live in a home. What he needed was an office cleaner.

Although Josie's social network was tiny in comparison to Dan's, her few friends provided her with more emotional warmth and support than his many acquaintances. On visiting his apartment, Josie instinctively sensed Dan's emotionally barren life and recoiled from it.

HOW MANY FAMILY MEMBERS are you in frequent contact with? How many friends do you have? How much do you participate in group activities? Do you live alone? Are you single or married? Do you experience marital problems? Do you have a significant other or life partner? Do you have children that you're in contact with? Certainly, the answers to these questions don't always paint an accurate picture, because relationships are more complex than these questions acknowledge. But these questions are a roundabout way of asking two other questions that really matter: Are you socially isolated? Do you lack social support? A network of strong, positive relationships brings personal joy, and it may also yield an unexpected dividend in better cardiovascular health. This chapter investigates an important heart-mind conspirator: social isolation and lack of social support.

The Pros and Cons of Social Attachment

The inevitable biological, psychological, socioeconomic, and environmental changes in human life cumulatively contribute to your stress level, and the higher your stress level, the more prone to illness you become. What scientists call the *social attachment strategy* means that you have a better chance of surviving stress if you're interacting with other humans—particularly if you form *intensive* attachments—rather than going through life as a solitary individual. Nurturance, social intimacy, affiliation, and attachment are key essentials for your physical and psychological health throughout your life.

How Social Relationships Protect You

Social relationships form a network, and in relationships, quality is more important than quantity. Your social network can be graded according to the numbers of voluntary associations with friends that you have. Although social relationships provide social support, it's clear that not all relationships are supportive. Affirmative social interactions are those in which you experience both autonomy and relatedness; these are the healthiest of interactions because they permit you to develop as a person within your familiar social settings.

Your physiology and psychology are influenced by how you develop within your social environment. Your family, the social system in which you were raised, and the organizations in which you participate influence your mind and body. Things that directly affect your health or influence health-related behavior can occur on several different levels. According to an Institute of Medicine report, the level of your social integration, the quality of your social ties, and the breadth and depth of your social support can be critical to your health.

People with positive relationships—that is, those with strong ties to family during childhood and intimacy with a spouse or friends during adulthood—have a lower stress load than those with minimal relationships. People who are socially isolated have been found to have higher blood pressure, higher blood levels of catecholamines, and changes in their cellular and antibody immune functions. The protective effect that social relationships have on health is known as *buffering*. Researchers have found that people without social buffers—such as those who are lonely—have lower immune function under stress. Other researchers have shown that this is especially true when people are going though major life transitions, such as experiencing loss (e.g., losing a spouse) or assuming new responsibility (e.g., the birth of a child). A social network and social support influence the coping process, thereby buffering the increase in stress load caused by the changes and improving one's resiliency to stress. An interesting effect of this increase in resiliency, stemming from one's attachments to social supports, is that the individual often has the reserve energy and motivation to help others in an altruistic way.

Another way that social support can influence health is through the promotion of health-enhancing behaviors. Influential individuals in your life can promote and encourage positive health practices.

Some Drawbacks of Social Networks

When you are part of a social network, of course, there can be harmful as well as beneficial consequences. Not all social ties are beneficial, and sometimes, being part of a tightly knit group can result in a limited array of resources. In addition, while strong relationships act as a buffer against the effects of adversity—such as those from socioeconomic setbacks—they can also result in situations such as divorce and bereavement that can reduce your sense of belonging and increase your fear of loneliness, often resulting in adverse health consequences. Some people also find themselves in relationships that are characterized by loneliness and depression—such as in families marked by anger, conflict, abuse, or violence—and find themselves more prone to illness. Finally, certain kinds of parent-child relationships, especially those in which parents are overly controlling, can be damaging to health.

How Relationships Can Directly Affect Your Health

There can be no doubt that significant social relationships have emotional benefits and a positive consequence of improved health. When you have positive relationships, including healthy and beneficial ties with family, you have reduced stress. The opposite is likely to be true if you have minimal or negative relationships.

Buffering Against Stress

At some point during your education or career, you have probably felt the stress of having to make a speech, which normally would not kill you. However, it is known that if you have coronary artery disease, making a speech about yourself increases your risk of having a heart attack. Researchers tested whether social support could help protect people who had to make such a speech; they had people make this speech under three different social situations and immediately afterward measured their systolic blood pressure. The three social situations consisted of the following:

- Giving the speech alone
- Giving the speech in the presence of a nonsupportive colleague
- Giving the speech in the presence of a supportive colleague

Those in the third situation showed the smallest increase in systolic blood pressure, followed by those who gave their speeches alone. Nonsupportive relationships, then, were shown to cause the most physiological stress.

Slowing the Progress of Ailments

The presence or absence of social support can change physiological processes. For example, in a study of middle-aged men with athero-sclerosis (the narrowing of one or more of the coronary arteries, obstructing the flow of blood), researchers found greater thickening of the carotid arteries in men who lived alone than in those who lived with their spouses.

Protecting You from Depression's Toxic Effects

If you have a heart condition and are presently depressed, you realize by now that you have reason to be concerned. But what if you also have family and friends who offer you lots of emotional support? Will that help ease the negative effects of depression on your cardiac health?

In a Canadian study of 887 men and women who had just survived a heart attack, researchers found no direct link between social support and survival. However, they did find that depressed patients with a high level of social support did not experience the increased mortality risk associated with depression. In other words, plentiful social support may neutralize the toxic effects of depression on the heart. In addition, high levels of social support predicted a lessening of depressive symptoms during the first year after the heart attack—a critical recovery period.

Women with coronary artery disease are regularly reported to have a poorer outcome than men with similar conditions. Social isolation and depression have been suggested as two of the causes. To test this theory, researchers assessed 292 Swedish women, between thirty and sixty-five years old, hospitalized for an acute coronary event. The women were assessed for social integration and depressive symptoms between three and six months after hospital admission, and their health was followed up for five years, with these results:

- Women with two or more depressive symptoms and a lack of social integration had the greatest risk of suffering further cardiac events.
- Women who were socially integrated and not depressed had the least risk.

- Women with the lowest social integration had a 2.3 times greater risk of further cardiac events than women with the highest social integration.
- Women with two or more depressive symptoms had a 1.9 times greater risk of cardiac events than women with one or no depressive symptoms.

Decreasing the Risk of Death

In studying how psychosocial variables might be linked to death in survivors of a heart attack, researchers interviewed 2,320 male survivors who were all participants in a beta-blocker (heart medication) heart attack trial. The study revealed that men who were both socially isolated and subject to high stress had more than four times the mortality risk of men with low levels of both isolation and stress. The researchers also found evidence linking the participants' level of education in that the greatest isolation and highest stress were most prevalent among the least-educated men and least prevalent among the best-educated men. And perhaps some of these results are due to the healthier lifestyles of those with stronger social relationships.

Over the past twenty years, thirteen large-scale studies have shown that people who are isolated have an increased risk of dying prematurely. According to the Institute of Medicine, social ties—especially deep and supportive relationships and the emotional support provided by them—increase the survival rate of people with serious cardiovascular disease and improve their medical outlook.

Encouraging a Healthier Lifestyle

Health-enhancing behaviors and social relationships were the focus of a study of 19,557 participants, aged eighteen years and older. Adjustments were made for age, sex, race, educational attainment, marital status, and employment status. Those with more solid social relationships were found to do the following:

- Smoke fewer cigarettes
- Have had blood pressure checked during the preceding year

- Have had cholesterol checked during the preceding year
- Engage in physical activity
- Eat a healthy diet, with recommended amounts of fruits and vegetables

Recognizing the Potential Benefit of Spiritual Support

Doctors have long noticed that people with religious beliefs generally seem to have better health than those without. Many doctors assumed that this was because religious people tended to lead stable, low-key lives and have few health-endangering habits. However, even this assumption does not explain the full extent of the health enhancement that religious people may receive. A survey of 92,909 people found that those who attended church weekly had half the death rate from coronary artery disease of those who didn't. More recent studies in the past decade over the health benefits of religious involvement include the following examples.

- Residents of Alameda County, California, who frequently attended places of worship had a lower death rate than residents who didn't.
- In Israel, residents of a religious kibbutz were found to have a 40 percent lower death rate from coronary artery disease over sixteen years than residents of a similar secular kibbutz.
- At six months after coronary artery bypass surgery, the death rate was significantly lower in patients with strong religious faith than in patients who were not religious.

While some behavioral scientists have questioned the strength of the association between health and religion, citing methodological flaws in many of the studies, a review of methodologically sound studies came to an interesting conclusion. It found that the health benefits of private worship—such as praying or reading scripture by yourself—appeared to be weaker than those of attending religious services with other people and thereby gaining social support. One way that spirituality might affect your health is through buffering your body's exaggerated response to stress. Such an exaggerated stress response can threaten your health. But belief, optimism, and emotional relaxation engender a positive emotional state, which in turn dampens the effects of your exaggerated stress response. Such positive emotional states also perpetuate healthy perceptions and physical well-being. Nevertheless, as the Institute of Medicine points out, the field of health and religious effects is relatively new and more research will be needed to determine potential associations and causalities.

Many doctor-patient relationships share distinct features with a faith-based community. These features include optimism and belief and the subtle use of the emotional relaxation response in thought or behavior. Frequently, the overall effects are repetitive healthy behaviors and a break in the chain of everyday or troubled thinking. When a state of solace—as opposed to stress—is embraced, the results may include positive health-promoting effects on organs and tissues. The heart is in a particular position to benefit, given its close communication with the visceral and emotional areas of the brain.

Engaging in Group Activities for Better Heart Health

We recommend participating in groups that are characterized by mutual support and in which competition is minimized. Many groups fit this profile quite well. Most religious groups are excellent examples, and so are a multitude of other supportive groups. These range from charitable community organizations like the Lion's Club to amateur athletic teams to therapeutic groups like Alcoholics Anonymous. If you have cardiac disease, cardiac rehabilitation groups and exercise clubs are excellent places to initiate this process. The Zipper Club, whose members have had cardiac surgery—and other groups for those who have automatic implantable cardioverter-defibrillators—play a positive role in bringing people together with shared experiences. Of course, the intimate social support provided by spouses, children, other relatives, and friends is most important to the healing of the individual suffering with any medical illness.

10

Two Stress Conspirators

NATURE GIVES YOUR BODY powerful means of responding to stress, but these stress responses can also hurt the heart and circulatory systems. Recently, the concept of allostasis has been introduced into the field of stress medicine. Allostasis—literally meaning "maintaining stability or homeostasis through change"—refers to the capacity to constantly adapt to changing internal and external environmental events. Your body's metabolism is kept in dynamic balance by the active brain. However, with repeated cycles of allostatic stress responses, an overwhelmingly stressful experience, or the inefficient turning on or shutting off of these allostatic processes, your body suffers a certain amount of metabolic wear and tear. This is the price you pay for adaptation, and it has been called *allostatic loading*. When it grows large, you become vulnerable to disease.

In this chapter, we look at two different types of stress that may contribute to allostatic loading: chronic (or subacute) stress and acute life stress. Before discussing these key conspirators, it is first important to understand your nervous system and how it responds to stress.

Your Autonomic Nervous System

Stress and the other negative emotions that we call heart-mind conspirators share several common pathways in affecting your body. One pathway is made up of a complex network of nerves called the *autonomic nervous system*. In humans, the autonomic nervous system controls the functions of the bodily organs and tissues without our conscious awareness. These nerves help control heartbeat, arterial blood pressure, breathing, hormonal secretions, gastrointestinal secretions and motility, bladder emptying, body temperature, and sweating, among other activities. The autonomic nervous system is wholly responsible for some of these activities and partially responsible for others. This system can affect your body with amazing intensity and speed as seen in the examples in the following list.

- Your heartbeat rate can double in three to five seconds.
- Your arterial blood pressure can double in ten to fifteen seconds.
- Your arterial blood pressure can drop low enough within four to five seconds for you to faint.
- You can break into a sweat in seconds.
- Your bladder can involuntarily empty in seconds.
- Your innermost reactions can show up on a lie detector polygraph.

Under stress, your sympathetic nervous system reacts and your body secretes catecholamines into your bloodstream, your heart beats faster and pumps a greater volume of blood, and your blood pressure rises. Such body changes can directly trigger lethal arrhythmias of your heart or possibly promote atherosclerosis in your coronary arteries. In people who already have coronary artery disease, these stress-induced body changes can cause a heart attack or other cardiac events. At the same time, stress will affect the hypothalamic-pituitary-adrenal cortical axis, leading to an outpouring of cortisol—a glucocorticoid that over time will reduce your body's sensitivity to insulin, predisposing susceptible individuals to type 2 diabetes mellitus.

A condition called *metabolic syndrome* is becoming more common in our stressed-out society. It consists of obesity, insulin resistance, hypertension, and elevated cholesterol and tryglyceride levels. Obviously, metabolic syndrome will increase a person's risk of heart disease.

Life Stress

Life stress is the kind of stress you are likely to undergo in your everyday activities. Stressors cause you to feel distress, and they range from daily hassles, physical ailments, and emotion (like anger and rage) to marital or family discord, worker or supervisor conflict, and general lack of support. Stressors can be physical (being in a low-temperature place), mental (doing arithmetic under time pressure), or emotional (having anxiety). Stressors cause you to feel emotional or psychological distress, and this distress is likely to result in physical symptoms that you may or may not connect with as its cause.

Stressors affect people differently. The same stressor that causes distress in your friend may cause you no distress. Similarly, the same stressor can cause different amounts of distress in you at different times. In turn, distress can cause various symptoms or varying degrees of the same symptoms in different people. You probably know people who seem prone to illness from distress and others who seem immune.

Chronic (Subacute) Life Stress

Chronic (or subacute) life stress is stress that happens repeatedly in your life. It consists of the accumulation of the effects of relatively unimportant stressful events over a period of months and often produces fatigue, lack of energy, increased irritability, and demoralization. Your stress level can build from a series of seemingly minor events, somewhat similar to the way relatively minor electrical charges can be stored and build up the power of a battery. Some examples of such an event are anticipation of a dental appointment or being caught in a lengthy traffic delay. While of greater magnitude, divorce and job loss are also common chronic stresses—although the events themselves may seem sudden, they usually occur with a buildup of stress over time.

Researchers have noted a buildup of minor stressful events in people before they suffer cardiac events, including heart attacks. This may be attributable to an elevation in allostatic loading. Chronic stress also raises the blood level of the PAI-1 antigen in healthy middle-aged men. High blood levels of this antigen increase the likelihood of fibrin deposition inside arteries, contributing to atherosclerosis.

Physical and mental stresses in daily life act as triggers of ischemia (the cutting off of blood flow to tissue) in people with coronary artery disease. When someone has ischemia of his or her heart muscles, the classical symptom is chest pain or angina. The likelihood of ischemia is greatest during intense physical activities and during stressful mental activities, as well as at times of anger. Frustration, tension, and sadness are also significant daily life triggers of ischemia in people with coronary artery disease.

In fact, in one study, coronary disease patients developed almost as much ischemia when speaking before an audience (a mental stress) as they did when subjected to a standard exercise stress test (physical stress). Because doctors use exercise tests to detect coronary artery disease in patients, researchers wondered if tests relying on physical stress—such as an exercise test—would detect people vulnerable to mental stress. They found that people who tested positive for coronary artery disease in exercise tests were also at high risk of developing ischemia from mental stress. This was found to apply also to marital stress.

Work-related stress is the most widely studied kind of chronic stress. At first, researchers focused mostly on work tension and job strain, which results from jobs with high demand and low decision-making abilities. One study of 1,928 men over six years found that job strain was linked to a fourfold increase in the risk of death due to cardiovascular causes.

Another kind of work-related stress comes from jobs with high demand and low reward. Stress from such jobs is a reliable predictor of cardiac events and has been connected to progression of atherosclerosis in the carotid arteries. Low job control in itself has been found to be a risk factor for cardiac events. These and other studies taken together suggest a strong association and a possible causal relationship between work-related chronic stress and coronary artery disease.

Interestingly, high-stress jobs significantly increase the risk of atherosclerosis in men between forty and sixty, but women the same age do not seem to be as affected. This conclusion was reached after 467 men and women were tested over eighteen months. Of men with the highest stress jobs, more than a third had atherosclerotic damage of the carotid arteries.

Acute Life Stress

As we mentioned earlier, major daily life stresses—such as bereavement, divorce, and job loss—may not be considered to be acute stress, no matter how sudden or intense they seem at the moment. However, some people do suffer a fatal heart attack or sudden cardiac death in response to sudden major psychological stresses that qualify as acute stress, such as an earthquake. The following reports provide strong evidence that acute stress can precipitate a heart attack or sudden cardiac death.

In 1981, Athens, Greece, suffered an earthquake measuring 6.7 on the Richter scale. Thirteen strong earthquakes were felt over the next twenty-four hours, with another four in the subsequent two days. In Athens at that time, the average number of deaths per day from coronary artery disease was 2.6. The numbers of deaths from coronary artery disease over the three days after the first earthquake were five, seven, and eight.

In 1994, one of the strongest earthquakes ever recorded in a big American city jolted millions of people awake in Northridge, in Los Angeles County, California. Before the earthquake, the average number of deaths per day from sudden cardiac death was 4.6. On the day of the earthquake, twenty-four people died from sudden cardiac death. After the earthquake, the average declined to 2.7. Of the twenty-four who died from sudden cardiac death, thirteen had symptoms—mostly chest pain—that started within an hour of the earthquake. The other eleven had no symptoms. Of the twenty-four deaths, only three were associated with physical exertion.

In 1995, a 7.2 earthquake struck Kobe City and five nearby cities in Japan. The casualties and damage were much greater than in most other earthquakes. For example, the Northridge earthquake killed 61 people, injured 7,000, and left 50,000 homeless. The 1995 Kobe earthquake killed about 6,000, injured 37,000, and left 310,000 homeless. The number of heart attack deaths during a three-month interval in 1995 for the earthquake area was 546, more than twice the 1994 number of 266. The number remained elevated at 354 even in 1996. There

Sympathetic Nervous System Hyperresponsivity

While sympathetic nervous system hyperresponsivity is different from acute stress, it does affect the heart similarly. This hyperresponsivity is a personal disposition in which you respond to stimuli in an exaggerated way with a quickened heartbeat and rise in blood pressure. The stimuli you respond to may be pleasant, challenging, or unpleasant. This hyperresponsivity is also known as *cardiovascular reactivity*. If this is the case, you must see a physician for an interview and physical examination. Your doctor will also search for possible medical causes (such as hyperthyroidism, other hormonal diseases, respiratory illnesses, and cardiac diseases).

When you have this disposition, you are known as a hot reactor, as distinct from a cold reactor, who does not experience this quickened heartbeat and rise in blood pressure. A hot reactor's more substantial and more frequent sympathetic nervous system responses can promote atherosclerosis over time.

Four studies used serial carotid Doppler measurements to investigate the effect of sympathetic nervous system hyperresponsivity on atherosclerotic plaque formation. All four studies found that atherosclerosis of the carotid arteries is more common in people who are hot reactors.

were wide variations in the heart attack death rates in different localities. As might be expected, the residents of completely destroyed houses suffered more heart attacks than other people. This means that chronic stress must also have played a contributory role in the high heart attack death rate that persisted even one year after the major earthquake in some districts.

Even with this strong evidence, you may wonder how an acute stress can result in a lethal cardiac event. Acute emotional stress stimulates an outpouring of catecholamines from the sympathetic nervous system. This can lead to rupture of an atherosclerotic plaque, clot formation inside a blood vessel, spasm of a coronary artery, or direct stimulation of heart muscles. Each of these physiological processes can act alone or together to initiate a heart attack and/or lethal arrhythmia. Fear can also lower the heart's threshold for rhythm disturbances.

Coping Mechanisms for Stress

When you come up against an acute life stress, you need to overcome a crisis. You must handle a number of adaptive tasks in the best way possible. Some of your coping mechanisms will prove to be mature and adaptive. Such coping mechanisms include developing awareness of self and others, sublimating anxieties in the service of making a contribution no matter what situation one finds oneself in, behaving altruistically, and intellectualizing by learning as much as possible about your problem without becoming obsessed about it. A certain amount of healthy denial that prevents a cardiac neurosis and doesn't prevent proper medical care can be helpful.

However, some coping mechanisms may also employ maladaptive and ultimately more stress-provoking mechanisms. These include experiencing denial that hinders medical attention, regressing into overdependency, projecting anger onto others, interpreting illness as punishment, and inciting loved ones to assume your own distress. Counseling is necessary when these maladaptive strategies are employed because they can lead to poor cardiac outcomes.

Managing Stress

The anxiety accompanying acute stress sometimes requires a short course of treatment with antianxiety medications such as benzodiazepines—for example, lorazepam (Ativan), diazepam (Valium), or alprazolam (Xanax).

However, medications should not be the only treatment. Stress-management interventions can be divided into behavioral strategies and coping mechanisms. Behavioral strategies may include breathing exercises, relaxation training, biofeedback and biofeedback-assisted relaxation, cognitive restructuring, and exercise, especially of the aer-

Giving Up Cigarettes

Cigarette smoking, in the context of stress, is a great health hazard not only in terms of cardiovascular disease but also in terms of cancers and pulmonary diseases. Many people smoke to relieve stress or depression, which is complicated by addiction to nicotine and withdrawal symptoms. Two-thirds of those seeking to quit resume smoking within three months. Behavioral counseling and nicotine replacement are the two most common forms of therapy. The former usually takes place in a smoking-cessation clinic and involves education, training, support, and practice. Identifying cues and triggers, practicing self-monitoring, and anticipating, along with skills training, are keys to success. Nicotine-replacement therapy is used with addicted individuals showing signs of withdrawal. Nicotine transdermal skin patches, chewing gum, and nasal sprays are used. The most effective approach combines the nicotine skin patch with behavioral therapy. Acupuncture has not been shown to be effective, and hypnosis is about as good as behavioral therapy alone. Because nicotine addiction shares features of opiate addiction, future research may involve the use of the opiate antagonist naltrexone to treat those with nicotine addiction.

obic type. Coping mechanisms include effective time-management and assertiveness training. These coping strategies are also effective ways to battle chronic stress.

Crisis intervention with a physician, psychologist, social worker, or pastoral counselor can also lower the risk of acute stress. Marshaling of your own strengths and assets through support, guidance, relaxation training, and network building is the goal, with resultant heightening of confidence and lowering of vulnerability. We talk more about many of these treatments in Part III.

11

Panic Disorder

When Fear Takes Hold

Mark, thirty-six, a computer programmer in Seattle, Washington, jogged regularly, worked out at the gym at least three times each week, and stayed on a well-balanced diet. About six months ago, he divorced his wife after a brief marriage. At the office, he was talking with several coworkers when he quickly developed an overwhelming fear and uncomfortable feeling. He had severe left-sided chest pain, together with difficulty in breathing, palpitations, and profuse sweating. The pain was so severe that Mark thought it was a heart attack. His symptoms subsided within thirty minutes, and all of his tests were normal in the emergency room. After a heart attack was ruled out, based on his symptoms, the emergency room doctor made a diagnosis of panic attack. On further probing, Mark remembered having several similar, brief episodes of unexpected fear, although not as intense, since the divorce. Mark's mother also had a history of panic attacks, and his father had undergone coronary bypass surgery four years earlier.

Deborah, twenty-six, had intermittent left-sided chest pain for a year but thought she was too young to have coronary artery disease. She was right. Working full time during the day at a major airline and going to law school at night gave Deborah a good excuse to postpone seeing her family doctor. But her last attack of chest pain was so severe, she finally broke down and went to him. She described her chest pain as being almost always accompanied by pounding in the chest, sweating, and difficulty in catching her breath. She also felt very anxious, and on several occasions she had an uncontrollable fear of dying or that something was terribly wrong. Most of the episodes were not associated with any particular event or activity, but at least three attacks came on while she was riding in a crowded bus. When giving her medical history, she told her doctor that she smoked a pack of cigarettes over the course of a week and drank two or three cups of coffee daily. When listening to her heart, her doctor heard a faint murmur suspicious of mitral valve prolapse, an abnormality of the valve between the upper and lower chambers on the left side of the heart. All her blood tests were normal, as was her electrocardiogram. An echo of her heart confirmed mitral valve prolapse, but there was no leakage (regurgitation) across the valve.

THE INTENSE FEAR, chest pain, pounding heart, and shortness of breath of a panic attack felt by both Mark and Deborah are frequently mistaken for angina or a heart attack. People with a panic attack are often not sure what they have, attribute the symptoms to something else, or ignore them outright. So far, research does not confirm panic disorder as a risk factor in coronary artery disease, but panic disorder may be associated with symptoms that are frequently confused as coronary artery disease.

A panic attack usually comes on quickly and is brief, and the whole episode lasts about thirty minutes. Typically no physical side effects ensue after a panic attack. The primary symptom is an intense fear or discomfort, and the intensity can vary with each attack. There are several common characteristic fears: fear of dying, fear of a heart attack, fear of going crazy, or fear of losing control. Many have a feeling of impending doom and a strong urge to flee, thus the aptly named *panic attack.*

Symptoms of Panic Disorder and How It Develops

What makes a panic attack a panic disorder? A panic attack by itself is not necessarily abnormal; a perfectly healthy person can have a rare, isolated panic attack. The most important feature is the presence of repetitive panic attacks: at least two attacks are required to diagnose a disorder, although most sufferers have many more. The frequency can vary from daily (during the course of a week) to occurrences separated by longer intervals of weeks to months.

Another important feature is that the panic attacks are mostly unexpected and spontaneous. In some people, the panic attack is triggered by a specific situation or location—referred to as a *situational panic attack*. Riding in an elevator, bus, train, or airplane are some common triggers. A panic attack can also happen spontaneously without any obvious trigger—called a *spontaneous* or *unexpected panic attack*. It is not necessary for the same trigger to bring on a panic attack every time. Some people have a mixture of both situational and unexpected panic attacks.

Besides the emotional feeling of intense fear, panic disorder is associated with at least four of the following common physical symptoms:

- Chest pain
- Palpitation, pounding heart, or rapid heartbeat
- Difficulty with breathing or a sensation of suffocation
- Dizziness, light-headedness, or fainting
- Sweating
- Trembling or shaking
- Sensation of pins and needles, and numbness
- Chills, blushing, or hot flushes
- Abdominal symptoms, including nausea, vomiting, and gastrointestinal upset
- Feelings of unrealness or detachment from oneself (depersonalization or derealization)

Panic disorder develops rapidly and typically peaks within ten minutes. Additionally, a condition known as a *limited-symptom panic attack* involves only one or two of the previously listed symptoms but still happens repeatedly.

People with panic disorder naturally are apprehensive about having another panic attack. They are concerned about their condition or are anxious about the physical consequences. The worry can be intense, often lasting more than a month, to the point of affecting their interpersonal relationships and job. Panic disorder is also twice as frequent in women as in men, and it mostly affects people from their late teens to forties.

Panic disorder is categorized either with or without agoraphobia— the fear of being in a certain location or situation that is uncomfortable and difficult to escape. (Refer to Chapter 7 for more on this fear.) Accordingly, these people try to avoid such locations or situations, such as being alone outside the home or riding in an airplane or on a bus or train.

Many people with panic disorder also have other conditions. At least half have a history of depression, with major depression being most common. Depressive disorders occur in 30 to 90 percent of those who commit suicide, and approximately 20 percent of suicides involve panic disorder. Researchers believe that the combination of depression and panic disorder conveys a greater suicide risk than either condition alone. Problems with substance abuse are also common in suicide.

Panic Disorder and Chest Pain

People with panic disorder often go to the emergency department or their primary care doctor for medical attention for physical symptoms rather than for intense fear or some other psychological complaints. Not surprisingly, many people with panic disorder undergo a long and costly evaluation for chest pain or are evaluated repeatedly in the emergency room or doctor's office, while the underlying panic disorder remains undiagnosed and untreated.

Most of the physical symptoms in panic disorders are related to the heart. When someone says "chest pain," doctors will usually think of heart disease, angina, or heart attack. Only during the past few years have physicians come to realize how common panic disorder is among people with heart complaints, particularly those seeking medical attention for chest pain.

One study found panic disorder to be the number one cause of noncardiac chest pain at a heart clinic. Another study reported an incidence of panic disorder greater than 35 percent among a group of 199 patients without known heart disease who had chest pain. A Canadian doctor found that the incidence of panic disorder ranged from 10 to

50 percent among patients with chest pain seen at cardiology clinics and in those with confirmed coronary artery disease. These reports have one important message: panic disorder is a common cause of chest pain. Yet differentiating the chest pain from coronary artery disease, panic disorder, and other causes is difficult, so don't try to do this yourself. You need the help of a doctor.

The cause of chest pain in panic disorder is not always clear. Some people clearly have concurrent coronary artery disease. Coronary spasm has also been speculated upon as a cause, but thus far there is little supporting evidence. In addition, the chest pain in panic disorder is not easy to study because the timing of a panic attack is so unpredictable.

While people suffering from panic disorder want to avoid unnecessary visits to the emergency room and doctor's office for extensive, repeated evaluations of chest pain, they often should have an initial evaluation to eliminate coronary artery disease. The doctor makes this judgment together with the patient. The decision is based on the age of the person, features of the chest pain, risk factors for heart disease, and other considerations. If indicated, an exercise stress test is a good starting point; reassurance and education are always helpful.

Panic Disorder and Mitral Valve Prolapse

Some people with panic disorder also have mitral valve prolapse (a malfunction of the valve between the upper and lower chamber on the heart's left side). Mitral valve prolapse has become the most common abnormal heart valve condition. About 3 to 4 percent of the population has the condition, and the percentage is higher in women. The severity of mitral valve prolapse covers a broad spectrum: many cases are inconsequential and may represent anatomical variants of a normal valve, but some cases are so severe that they require surgical replacement.

A Review of Mitral Valve Prolapse

As illustrated in Figure 11.1, the mitral valve is located on the left side of the heart and separates the left ventricle from the left atrium. The valve functions like a partition: it opens when blood moves from the

left atrium into the left ventricle and closes when the left ventricle contracts and pumps blood out of the heart. If the valve is functioning normally, there should be no leakage of blood back into the left atrium
during contraction of the left ventricle.

In mitral valve prolapse, the valve balloons into the left atrium like
the dome of a parachute when the left ventricle contracts. In most
cases, mitral valve prolapse is of no consequence as long as there is no
leakage of blood back into the left atrium.

However, mitral valve prolapse is not always a benign condition.
In some cases, it can be so severe that the valve no longer functions as
an effective partition. People with this condition have leakage of blood
back into the left atrium when the left ventricle contracts. Doctors call
this *mitral regurgitation* or *mitral valve insufficiency*. Mitral valve
prolapse is one of many conditions that can cause mitral regurgitation.
Over time, a leaking valve can lead to heart failure, and the valve needs
to be repaired or replaced. When a leaky valve is present, it increases
the risk of endocarditis, an infection of the heart valve. Mitral valve
prolapse is also a cause for arrhythmia.

Figure 11.1

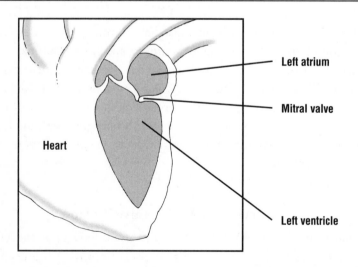

The mitral valve opens when blood moves into the left ventricle and closes when blood is
ejected from the left ventricle.

The symptoms of mitral valve prolapse are mostly related to the heart: chest pain, palpitation, shortness of breath, and fainting. These symptoms are similar to the physical symptoms in anxiety disorders, particularly panic disorder.

Is There a Connection?

Many patients with mitral valve prolapse also have a history of panic disorder. In fact, panic disorder and mitral valve prolapse share a similar age and gender distribution. Many of the symptoms, such as chest pain, shortness of breath, and palpitations, are similar for both conditions. This is where the agreement ends.

Of the many reports on panic disorders and mitral valve prolapse, some claimed an association between the two conditions and others saw no association. One review concluded that mitral valve prolapse and panic disorder may coexist in the same patient, but the two conditions don't have a positive or negative effect on each other or share a causal relationship. Another group of psychiatrists and cardiologists in Taiwan also concluded that panic attacks had no significant effect on mitral valve prolapse.

On the other hand, a study of twenty patients with panic disorder and mitral valve prolapse reported an improvement in the mitral valve prolapse after treatment of the panic disorder. In another study, a hundred patients undergoing heart catheterization for suspected coronary artery disease were interviewed. Major depression, panic disorder, or both were more common among those with suspected coronary artery disease. A second finding was that there was an even greater frequency of major depression and panic disorder among those with normal coronary arteries but in the presence of mitral valve prolapse. In Japan, a doctor reported that mitral valve prolapse was twice as common in patients with panic disorder as in the healthy population.

Treating Panic Disorder

Although panic disorder is common in coronary artery disease (ranging from 10 to 50 percent in cardiology patients with documented coronary artery disease, according to researchers at the Montreal Heart Institute), it is unclear to what extent panic disorder confers risk or exacerbates cardiac disease. While panic disorder is different from depression and the other emotional conspirators in that it may not make heart disease more likely, its symptoms can also be confused with coronary artery disease. If you are making frequent visits to the emergency room or doctor's office for chest pain and other cardiac symptoms that are common in panic disorder, it's important to know that it can be treated in various ways.

Avoid Chemical and Herbal Triggers

Many chemical substances can bring on symptoms similar to a panic attack, including chest pain. Alcohol and caffeine in coffee, tea, and sodas are two cases in point. Some asthma medications, cold medicine, and diet pills contain synthetic compounds that can provoke an attack. Unknown to many, some herbs contain natural stimulants. If you suffer from panic attacks, you should limit the intake of these substances or avoid them completely. Women who are premenstrual or perimenopausal may find that stimulants are more likely to cause feelings of anxiety and panic.

Address Underlying Medical Conditions

Some medical conditions also have symptoms similar to a panic attack. Hyperactivity of the thyroid is one of the more common examples. Pulmonary diseases like emphysema and asthma may also cause panic symptoms.

Medications

There are excellent treatment strategies for panic disorder today. Treatment for panic disorder will also treat concurrent depression that is present. All of the selective serotonin receptor inhibitors, such as fluoxetine (brand name Prozac) or paroxetine (brand name Paxil), can provide effective control of panic disorder, with the benefit usually beginning within three to four weeks of treatment. They are considered the first-line treatment. Occasionally, changes in the SSRI being used or even a switch to another antidepressant—like the serotonin-norepinephrine reuptake inhibitors (SNRIs), such as venlafaxine (Effexor)—may be necessary. The medication needs to be taken continuously, however, and not just during an attack. The sedative clonazepam (Klonopin), which is a benzodiazepine, is sometimes added during the initial phase, before the SSRI takes effect, to reduce any temporary restlessness the SSRI may cause. We talk more about antidepressants in Chapter 14.

The duration of medication therapy depends on the individual and his or her panic disorder. Some may be on it for a year or less, while others need a longer period. It is important to try to get the best control of symptoms possible. Note that an abrupt withdrawal from SSRIs can cause a flu-like syndrome, and withdrawal from benzodiazepine sedatives after significant use can cause serious effects like confusion, changes in blood pressure and heart rate, and seizures.

Cognitive Behavior Therapy

Some doctors use behavior therapy, which includes breathing and relaxation exercises, as an important component of the treatment. Cognitive behavior therapy, which involves exercises to change automatic thoughts that lead to negative emotions and is often combined with relaxation training, is also used and can produce results comparable to drug therapy. For panic disorder, these are the central components of cognitive behavior therapy:

- Correction of cognitive misperception and automatic thinking and overresponsiveness to anxiety symptoms
- Breathing retraining and muscle relaxation
- Exposure and desensitization to anxiety-provoking situations

These approaches can give you the tools that you need to reduce or eliminate the number of attacks and to stop avoiding places or situations that bring on an attack.

12

Why So SAD?

Daily and Seasonal Rhythms

Janice had lived all her life in Portland, Maine. She loved the town, in spite of the long winters. Her daughters, who were in their late twenties and working in Atlanta, kept their visits home for Thanksgiving and Christmas short. Before coming home, they always wondered how bad things would be because their mother hated the whole holiday season. Janice's birthday was in mid-December—another year older—and her son (their brother) had been killed in a car accident a few years before in late November. Janice and her husband had since divorced, and she had never remarried.

Some years, in her daughters' estimation, Thanksgiving was not so bad, but, without fail, Christmas was awful. By then, the frequent glasses of wine Janice was drinking at Thanksgiving had changed to vodka and late-night rants and accusations. However, Janice always brightened when the crocuses and daffodils showed. She'd feel fine all spring and summer, until November rolled around.

One morning in mid-December following her fifty-sixth birthday, Janice had a mild heart attack while still in bed. Her neighbors rushed her, still in her pajamas, to the emergency room. After daylong tests and several days in the hospital for observation, Janice was discharged. Both daughters came up and stayed on for a week to take care of her.

While Janice was in the hospital, her daughters talked over the phone to their father, who lived in Las Vegas. They discovered that their mother had always become depressed beginning in November and was miserable until spring. She had been that way in the early years of her marriage—before their brother was killed in the car accident and long before her birthday age upset her. Her daughters revealed this fact to the cardiologist before Janice was released.

When they returned in February, they were pleasantly surprised to find their mother as well as she had claimed to be in recent phone calls. Janice wasn't drinking, and she was in a far better mood than the previous year. She said that in addition to her heart condition, she was being treated for seasonal affective disorder, which neither of her daughters had ever heard of.

AN EXQUISITELY SENSITIVE internal clock—the suprachiasmatic nucleus—residing in the middle of the brain manages our body on a twenty-four-hour cycle and a seasonal calendar. This clock is vital to our health, but it can also contribute to illness. Coronary artery disease, in fact, has seasonal and other time patterns. For example, more Americans die from heart attacks in the first week of each month; heart attacks, sudden cardiac death, and stroke are most frequent between the hours of 5:00 A.M. and 12:00 P.M.; and heart attacks are most frequent on Mondays and during winter. In addition, elsewhere in the world the following has been found:

- New Zealand heart attack survivors were most likely to have further cardiac symptoms on weekends and Mondays.
- Canadian deaths from heart attacks were almost one-fifth higher in January than in September.
- In Australia and New Zealand, coronary events—both fatal and nonfatal—were 20 to 40 percent more likely to occur during their winter (June to August) and spring (September to November) than in other seasons.

Why do so many people have a heart attack in the morning, and what are the possible causes behind more heart attacks and sudden death during the winter months? This short chapter answers those questions.

How the Time of Day Affects Your Heart

Early morning may be the time of day when you are relaxed and rested after a good night's sleep. You are probably not doing any strenuous activities. It's a time of the day when everything may still be calm and quiet. However, inside the body, the situation is quite different.

Early in the morning, your body has to undergo important changes to meet the physiological needs required after getting out of bed. Your body is revving up for a new day. Your blood pressure rises, your heart rate increases and pumps more forcefully, your body fuel diffuses into the bloodstream, and the blood is redirected to the muscles. These activities can lead to plaque rupture, platelet activation, clot formation, and irritability of the heart; and these alterations are the same mechanisms behind a heart attack and arrhythmia.

The Effects of Winter on Heart Disease

Because so many more heart attacks happen in winter, some researchers have suggested that major holidays during December and January play a significant role, such as in Janice's case. We agree that the stress and emotional highs and lows associated with these important holidays cannot be underestimated for many people. However, other factors also make a difference.

Low Temperatures

Environmental temperatures influence seasonal variations in deaths due to coronary artery disease. Lower temperatures can affect the heart by raising blood pressure, and cooling of the skin causes constriction of the blood vessels and initial decreases in cardiac output. Exposure to cold temperature is known to bring on angina in some people with known coronary artery disease. For example, in Britain, people's blood pressures in winter exceed those of summer by about 5 mmHg. This winter rise in blood pressure has been linked to a 20 percent rise in events leading to coronary artery disease. In addition, extreme drops or rises in temperature cause an increase in deaths due to coronary artery disease between one and four days after the temperature change occurs. For example, winter coronary artery disease mortality rises more in European regions with low standards of indoor heating, housing insulation, and winter clothing than in those with high standards.

However, studies have raised doubts about links between low winter temperatures and increased death rates from coronary artery disease. For example, seasonal variations occur in coronary artery disease death rates in subtropical areas, where temperature variations between winter and summer are negligible. In Hawaii, where seasonal variation in temperature is minimal, a 22 percent increase occurs in coronary artery disease deaths in winter. In Hong Kong, where temperature differences between winter-spring and summer-fall average only 8 degrees Celsius, a winter increase of 37 percent occurs in coronary artery disease deaths. Clearly, another explanation is needed.

Seasonal Affective Disorder (SAD)

Researcher Dr. Leo Sher offered an explanation of how depression could be linked to the seasonal pattern of coronary artery disease. He pointed out that many mood states also have a seasonal pattern. Seasonal affective disorder (SAD), a special form of depression that comes on during the fall and winter months, was cited as an example. As we have seen, a wealth of research has linked depression to coronary artery disease and myocardial infarction. Similarly, Dr. Sher suggested that a person with winter depression will be more susceptible to a heart attack during the fall and winter months.

SAD is regarded as a seasonal form of either major or minor depression or bipolar depression (manic depression). These regularly occurring symptoms of depression (excessive eating and sleeping, weight gain) usually develop during the fall or winter and remit in spring and summer months. A person is likely to be diagnosed with SAD when this happens over two successive years or several times over a single winter with no nonseasonal depression episodes. Some sufferers also develop a craving for sugary and/or starchy foods. With SAD, people feel depressed to various degrees. Most are depressed only during winter, but a small number of people become depressed in summer and recover in winter.

Finnish doctors estimate that one in one hundred people have a lifetime chance of getting SAD; however, they also note that informa-

The Role of Ultraviolet Light

Some researchers suggest that the level of ultraviolet radiation should be taken into account. Most of our body's vitamin D is synthesized by the skin after exposure to ultraviolet radiation from the sun. People with coronary artery disease tend to have lower levels of vitamin D. Therefore, the increased exposure to ultraviolet radiation in the summer may protect you from coronary artery disease.

tion is too vague for any truly reliable estimates to be made. Children are less liable to have SAD than adults, and there's little information on its prevalence among the elderly. More women than men are affected, but men are more likely to have SAD in the form of major depression, where women have it in the form of minor depression.

Researchers are not sure exactly what causes SAD. Decreasing length of daylight has the ability to trigger depression, but no particular decrease in daylight length has been found to be responsible. Thus we can't say for sure that when we lose two hours of daylight, SAD-prone people are going to be depressed.

How SAD Affects You

We can say with reasonable certainty, though, that your biological clock is involved in SAD. Your biological clock is governed by a tiny area, made up of about seventy thousand neurons, in the brain's hypothalamus. Called the *suprachiasmatic nucleus*, it processes external information in order to regulate body temperature, sleep/wake cycles, and secretion of hormones such as cortisol, melatonin, thyroxin, and vasopressin. In humans, the suprachiasmatic nucleus regulates a daily cycle that averages about twenty-four hours and eleven minutes. Light has a powerful effect on the process. A burst of light in the morning can advance the process, whereas a burst of light in the evening can delay it.

We know quite a bit about how our biological clock regulates our daily cycle. However, we know much less about how our biological clock itself changes with the seasons of the year. Seasonal fluctuations in body rhythm certainly do take place. For example, hormones and neurotransmitters associated with depression are more plentiful in the bloodstream at some times of year than at others.

Treating SAD

Psychiatrists treat people with SAD by exposure to strong light (called *phototherapy* or *bright light therapy*) for two hours each morning. This simulates an earlier sunrise, advances their biological clock, and has been shown to suppress the brain's secretion of melatonin. Many people respond to this treatment, though there have been no research findings to definitely link this therapy with an antidepressant effect. For mild symptoms, it may also be helpful to arrange your home and workplace so that it receives more sunlight or to spend more time outdoors during the day. If exposure to strong light doesn't work, an antidepressant drug may also prove to be helpful in reducing or eliminating SAD symptoms. However, it's important to discuss your symptoms thoroughly with your doctor before taking any action.

PART III

Combating the Heart-Mind Conspiracy

13

Survival Strategies
for Heart Patients

Mike, fifty-two, was a policeman and a father of three in San Diego. His health had been excellent, despite the fact that he smoked two packs a day. After his brother died of a massive heart attack, he went for a stress test, which was positive. Cardiac catheterization was scheduled, and his cardiologist diagnosed three-vessel coronary artery disease. A surgeon came to see him in the cath lab and persuaded him to have bypass surgery the next day. Mike thought there was no reason to delay surgery. He had bypass surgery the next day as planned, woke up within two hours in the intensive care unit, and was transferred to a regular hospital room the same day. He was home three days after his operation. His doctors congratulated him on a remarkably trouble-free bypass. Mike himself was impressed, as were his family and colleagues. What Mike didn't realize was that his nightmare was just beginning.

Even while in the hospital, Mike's terrible cough from his years of smoking came back, and he began suffering from nicotine withdrawal. By day five, his cough was so severe that his chest incision was hurting. Within another twenty-four hours, he noticed a cranberry juice–like drainage from the lower part of the incision. In the emergency room, the doctors found his chest incision had separated from the severe coughing, so he was brought back to the operating room where his incision was reclosed. His second hospital stay was complicated by pneumonia, wound infection, difficult pain control, and a severe bout of depression. He was in the hospital for more than four weeks.

A year later, Mike was a changed man. He was no longer working. His chest incision remained a source of daily discomfort, and he was angry at what had happened to him. Mike's case does not typify the usual open-heart patient. Most heart surgery patients undergo uncomplicated operations, are discharged from the hospital around seven days after surgery, and gradually make a recovery over a period of two to three months. Some people recover faster and some at a slower pace. It is important to recognize that everyone is different and does not fit one formula.

To GET THE BEST outcome from surgery, you need to find the right surgeon and hospital, but it doesn't stop there. You need to keep asking questions and stay involved. In previous sections, we discussed the interconnections between heart disease and emotions. In this chapter, we concentrate on what you can do to recover from heart surgery, and we provide some general principles and treatment approaches that we've used for our patients.

Before Surgery

There are preparations that you can make before a major operation like coronary artery bypass surgery. On a practical level, you need to be calm and in good spirits and have a good night's sleep before major surgery. Because this is not always possible, surgery frequently starts on a wrong footing.

You are likely to enter the hospital on the day of your surgery, perhaps at 6:00 A.M. or sometimes even earlier. Allowing an hour for travel, this may mean that you have to get up at 4:00 A.M. In addition, you may be anxious and have some trouble sleeping the night before, making you both physically and emotionally tired. You may have to wait hours for surgery in the hospital due to unexpected delays. This adds frustration and contributes to more anxiety. A common solution is to take a sleeping pill or something to calm your nerves. Is this the only answer?

Surviving Sudden Cardiac Death

One of the most frightening and traumatic experiences related to heart disease is surviving sudden cardiac death. People with malignant ventricular arrhythmias who have survived an episode of sudden death or who are at risk for it form a special group of cardiac patients. They have often gone through not only the experience of surviving sudden cardiac death episodes but also harrowing hospitalizations replete with intense electrophysiological studies (EPS), often culminating with the implantation of an automatic internal cardioverter-defibrillator (AICD). An EPS is a diagnostic test to investigate a person's rhythm disturbances. An AICD is an implantable device that electrically shocks someone with a life-threatening heart rhythm disturbance back into a stable rhythm. These patients may go on to suffer from depression, panic attacks, and post-traumatic stress disorder. This is more often the case when there are frequent AICD discharges, which can be harrowing and very painful. Fortunately, the newer devices include anti-tachycardia pacemakers that tend to discharge less frequently.

A close collaboration between a cardiologist and psychiatrist can be very helpful in care and recovery. One's heart doctor provides information optimistically: offering insight into the potential frustrations and eventual success of the EPS and AICD. Confidence increases and apprehension diminishes when a cardiologist spends time being supportive. A psychiatrist evaluates mental status and provides supportive therapy to strengthen coping. He or she can also provide cognitive behavioral therapy for mood disturbances such as depression and can prescribe medications—usually benzodiazepines and/or antidepressants—for mood disorders. The psychiatrist, nurse, or mental health assistant can also teach behavioral techniques such as relaxation response or autohypnosis. This approach offers patients a better sense of self-control over stressful situations and the difficult experiences they have gone through during their traumatic cardiac events.

One solution is to start going to sleep earlier a few days before the operation. Also, if you live far away from the hospital, consider staying in a hotel close to the hospital that last night. While you don't have to stop normal activities, it may be a good idea to slow down or take a break from work in the week or so before the surgery. People like to think of themselves as indispensable at the workplace, but this is seldom the case. Instead, it is more important that you take time for yourself.

A well-balanced diet is also helpful, but there is no need for special diets, vitamins, or dietary supplements before surgery. In fact, dietary supplements are ill advised, because they may contain substances that promote bleeding and interact with conventional medications. If you're at risk for heart disease, folic acid is usually recommended, because it can lower the blood level of homocysteine, a probable cardiac risk factor. Interestingly, folic acid deficiency can also potentially cause depressive symptoms.

Reactions to the Need for Surgery

A serious illness such as coronary artery disease frequently heralds the beginning of a major transitional phase for the patient. We see this in many heart surgery patients. The transitional phase almost always comes without warning or preparation. In the acute period of the illness, you not only have to recover from the illness but you also have to tackle important issues relating to family, employment versus retirement, potential disability, and a range of accompanying emotions.

Not surprisingly, the illness and subsequent surgery often lead to an internal crisis that can increase your vulnerability and diminish confidence. However, how you handle the crisis has a strong influence on your reactions to the illness, both physically and emotionally.

Making Adjustments

Coronary artery disease is a serious illness with both acute and chronic components. Those diagnosed with heart disease will need to make certain adjustments. For example, there may be physical adjustments, such as adjusting to angina or to a hospital environment. There may also be a need to adjust to a decreased level of functioning, to the invasive procedures used for evaluation and treatment, or to the many doctors with whom a patient will come in contact.

There are also personal adjustments, such as maintaining psychological equilibrium, maintaining a healthy measure of self-esteem, maintaining supportive attachments to family members and friends, and establishing a different perception of the future. On a more practical level, you should feel free to ask your physician the following questions:

- Will I have pain?
- Do I need surgery or other interventional procedures?
- Can I resume the same activities afterward?
- Can I return to work?
- Will my relationship with my spouse change?
- Will I ever return to my normal state?
- Will I survive the condition?

If you don't get straight answers, keep asking.

Healthy and Unhealthy Coping Mechanisms

Any adjustments to an illness require coping mechanisms, and different people use different ones.

Some people resort to denial, such as thinking that the illness is not all that serious. This may be all right as long as compliance with medical treatment is not jeopardized. Others suppress any uncomfortable emotions, such as fear and anger, which is generally not healthy. A few people use avoidance. A typical example of this is someone who states that it is impossible to take any time away from work for the necessary evaluation or treatment. This approach can jeopardize a person's health.

Some people seek out knowledge and medical information as an indication of self-reliance, or they try to master the technical procedures associated with the particular illness. This new knowledge often will add to patient confidence. Still others ask for solace from loved ones—and perhaps even from their medical caretakers. If the support is forthcoming, it can be very positive.

Taking Time to Heal

When people are hospitalized, they are always sent this message: get well soon; have a speedy recovery. It doesn't matter whether people are in the hospital for angina, a heart attack, or surgery, as it is always the same message. This get-well-quick exhortation comes in the form of greeting cards, balloons, flowers, and gifts. The emphasis is on speed, with patients almost feeling as if they are in a race.

Of course, patients should be encouraged to get out of bed to a chair and start moving about when appropriate. Rehabilitation from any illness is very important. But after a major operation or illness, you can't get the cells to divide any faster during the healing phase. Nor can collagen fibers be manufactured at a faster pace. Nature takes its course on its own time schedule. Get well, but take all the time you need to do so.

Your Doctor's Role: General Treatment Strategies for Cardiac Patients

The late Thomas Hackett and his successor, Ned Cassem, both psychiatrists from the Massachusetts General Hospital, established a general approach to the cardiac patient many years ago. These principles have weathered the test of time and are still applicable today. We use them in our practices when indicated.

For the cardiac patient's recovery, the following six steps are usually recommended:

1. Educate the cardiac patient, and dispel any damaging myths.

2. Help the cardiac patient to anticipate stress and other fears.
3. Use antianxiety and antidepressant medications when appropriate.
4. Promote physical conditioning and proper nutrition.
5. Teach behavioral approaches such as relaxation exercises, self-hypnosis, biofeedback, meditation, and cognitive behavioral therapy.
6. Involve patients, when appropriate, in psychotherapy such as supportive psychotherapy, interpersonal psychotherapy, cognitive behavioral psychotherapy, and group therapies to help people make better adjustments to heart disease.

For the cardiac patient's family, the following steps are recommended:

1. Provide information about heart disease to families.
2. Offer advice about family response to heart disease.
3. Serve as a resource for community support.
4. Help the patient and family make decisions that are based on risks and benefits.
5. Acknowledge the emotional responses of the family.
6. Stress that some adjustment to heart disease may be necessary as part of a long-term coping process.
7. Warn the patient and his or her family against making abrupt family changes.
8. Suggest and encourage periodic emotional and physical refueling for caretakers to avoid burnout.

Cardiac Rehabilitation

Cardiac rehabilitation is a prescribed set of activities designed to aid in the recovery of patients who have cardiac disease, with the goal of restoring them to the best level of functioning they can achieve. It includes an exercise prescription, nutritional guidance, lifestyle education, and relaxation and behavioral training. If you fall into one of these categories, you will benefit from cardiac rehabilitation:

- Heart attack
- Coronary bypass surgery or other open-heart procedures
- Balloon angioplasty and stent placement
- Chronic stable angina
- Chronic heart failure
- Heart transplantation

The goal of cardiac rehabilitation is to prevent future cardiac events, rehospitalization, and death from cardiac causes. Cardiac rehabilitation also has the potential to prevent disability due to cardiovascular disease. This is especially important in elderly people and those with occupations that involve intensive physical activity. Rehabilitation is accomplished through a program of exercise and interventions designed to modify cardiac risk factors. Exercise is also kown to be useful in reducing depressed and anxious moods; thus, exercise is an outstanding way to strengthen the heart-mind connection.

Benefits of Cardiac Rehabilitation

While cardiac rehabilitation has beneficial effects on lipids, weight loss, and exercise tolerance, many of its positive effects are actually psychological in nature. According to one study, anxiety, emotional stress, lack of self-esteem and self-confidence, depression, social isolation, and patient-reported quality of life all improved after cardiac rehabilitation. Other studies have reported that mortality rates drop by approximately 25 percent after cardiac rehabilitation.

Why do we see this significant improvement in mortality with cardiac rehab? We are not certain, but, in addition to improving cardiac exercise tolerance, addressing issues relating to depression and social isolation after a cardiac event during cardiac rehab may be partially responsible.

An increasing number of cardiac rehabilitation programs are incorporating mental health components. Usually this includes stress management, and specific psychosocial screening and interventions—such as cognitive behavioral therapy—are also provided in some programs. Psychiatric referrals are made when screenings reveal depression and other serious mental health conditions. Indeed, comprehensive cardiovascular rehabilitation provides an effective way to identify and treat mood disorders (such as depression) following cardiac events. Even cardiac rehabilitation programs without psychosocial intervention may have beneficial effects on depression in patients after major coronary events.

The benefits of cardiac rehab were recently reported in 338 patients who had suffered a major cardiac event four to six weeks earlier and who participated in cardiac rehabilitation consisting of thirty-six sessions over a three-month period. After cardiac rehab, depressed patients had marked improvements of depression scores and other behavioral parameters such as anxiety, hostility, and quality of life. These depressed patients also showed increased exercise capacity, reduced percentage of body fat, and decreased low-density lipoprotein cholesterol levels. Depression reduction may have been assisted by the effects of exercise on mood states, as well as through education of patients and their families and the benefit of social support.

What about cardiac rehab programs with built-in psychosocial components? One study showed that patients enrolled in programs that included psychosocial interventions had greater reductions in anxiety and depression, lower blood pressure, and lower rates of mortality and recurrent cardiac events at two years than those enrolled in programs without a psychosocial component.

Cardiac rehab often involves group-based behavioral interventions. These interventions target psychosocial factors and may improve prognosis in coronary artery disease. Because of these encouraging findings, the National Heart, Lung, and Blood Institute sponsored a large-scale clinical trial of psychosocial intervention (cognitive behavioral therapy and group therapy when feasible) called the Enhancing Recovery in Coronary Heart Disease (ENRICHD) study. This was the first large-scale multicenter randomized clinical trial of psychosocial intervention. It targeted depression and social isolation and aimed to reduce morbidity and mortality in coronary heart disease patients. While there were improvements in depression and social isolation, the intervention unfortunately did not improve cardiac-event-free survival.

On the other hand, highly structured group-based interventions consisting of eight sessions of training in various coping skills have been shown to decrease medical/surgical service costs and utilization from 15 to 20 percent in a group of high utilizers of medical services.

Benefits of Behavioral Intervention Programs

Successful group-based behavioral intervention programs share several qualities. The group settings are more efficient than one-on-one approaches and enable patients to learn from one another. Groups also serve as an important source of social support. Cognitive behavioral therapy combined with social skills training can provide patients with hands-on practice to manage stress-filled situations and the negative emotions that surface in them.

In addition, relaxation techniques, meditation, and progressive muscle relaxation, in combination with the increased awareness of symptoms that comes with the use of cognitive behavioral therapy skills, can help reduce autonomic nervous system arousal. Patients can also decrease troubling thoughts and emotions and reduce potentially dangerous sympathetic nervous system overarousal. Treatment can be limited to a fixed number of sessions, and often no more than six to eight sessions are required. Manuals and protocols effectively allow patients to learn about the skills involved. Through practice and homework, these skills can be mastered and maintained.

These strategies have a special focus on people who have suffered a heart attack or undergone open-heart surgery. They can help you improve your quality of life if you have heart disease. More research will be needed to establish whether following them may also help prevent the occurrence of a cardiac event in a high-risk person.

Now that we have explored some cardiac survival strategies, the next chapter focuses on specific treatments for depression—including medications and various behavioral therapies—to help you on the road to recovery.

14

Treating Depression and Helping the Heart

DOCTORS NOW HAVE various effective treatments for severe or major depression. Indeed, success with drug therapy for major depression (shown by at least a 50 percent reduction in depressed mood and other symptoms) has been reported in 55 to 65 percent of patients. Even if you are someone with less severe but more chronic depression—a condition called *dysthymia*—you may also improve with antidepressant treatments.

If you suffer from minor depression—which is characterized by a nonchronic depressed mood and fewer symptoms—and antidepressant treatments have not yet been shown to provide a clear-cut benefit, then supportive care and watchful waiting can be an option; but this decision is best guided by a psychiatrist. In this chapter, we discuss the treatment of depression and other negative emotions from the standpoint of someone with heart disease. We also discuss how to treat depression with and without medications.

Knowing When to Treat Depression

When should depression be treated? A doctor seeing someone with depression has to decide whether he or she will recover spontaneously (without treatment) during the next two to four weeks. In general, if

139

you have moderate to severe symptoms, substantial activity impairment, and a long duration (several weeks) of depression, you are unlikely to recover on your own until after many months, if at all, and thus treatment should be started. The presence of other psychiatric problems or of major stressors may point to the need for more aggressive management.

On the other hand, if you have new onset, less severe, and less persistent signs of depression, you may benefit from supportive therapy without medication. You will need to be reevaluated by your doctor in two to four weeks to assess your progress. Treatment should be started if symptoms persist after this period of watchful waiting.

What About Bereavement?

It can be difficult to distinguish normal mourning from bereavement that has deteriorated into depression. This is because people who are grieving have symptoms similar to major depression. Although treatment decisions should be individualized, a rough guideline is this: when grieving people have classic depressive symptoms for more than two months, they should be offered antidepressant therapy.

Discussing Thoughts of Suicide

Major depression is common among people who go on to commit suicide. The highest rate of suicide occurs among elderly white men, which is a group also particularly prone to coronary artery disease. Suicide in this group is up to six times higher than in the general population. Men are more likely to commit suicide than women, although women attempt it more. Thus, it is important to discuss these issues with your loved ones experiencing depression, even if it feels awkward. The best approach is to be specific. You can ask, "Do you ever think of hurting yourself or taking your own life?" Another approach might be, "Do you feel that life is not worth living?"

If the answer is yes, ask whether your loved one has a plan to commit suicide and if he or she knows what that plan might be. If you, as a friend or family member, feel uncomfortable asking these questions, seek the assistance of a professional, but do not avoid the issue. There is no truth to the myth that you suggest the idea of suicide by asking these kinds of questions. If you or a professional feel unsure of your loved one's resistance against suicidal urges or are concerned that he or she might harm him- or herself, emergency psychiatric evaluation must be sought immediately. The importance of reporting suicidal thoughts, particularly when they are becoming more intense or more frequent, must be emphasized.

Ruling Out Medical Illnesses That Can Cause or Mimic Depression

Making the diagnosis of depression is often not simple. Symptoms of depression are often intermingled with symptoms of other medical illnesses. For example, when a patient complains of weight loss or loss of energy in the setting of heart disease, the symptoms may be due to severe heart failure. The medical term for this condition is *cardiac cachexia*, which literally means heart starvation. A thorough medical history and physical examination are very valuable in confirming that depressive symptoms are due to depression.

Other physical illnesses that can have symptoms similar to depression include severe anemia, hypothyroidism, cancer, diabetes, cerebral vascular disease, and chronic medical illness. This diagnostic puzzle is particularly challenging in the elderly. Depression in this age group may signify a vascular depression, for example. Close monitoring of risk factors for cerebral vascular disease such as hypertension and diabetes is warranted, along with treatment of the depression.

At times, it can be very difficult to differentiate a medical illness with symptoms that mimic depression from actual depression brought on by the medical condition. Making this differentiation is important for treatment. For example, if tiredness is due to anemia, a blood transfusion or iron supplement may be necessary. If depression-like symptoms are due to hypothyroidism, a thyroid supplement may be needed. On the other hand, major depression secondary to medical illness can often respond to antidepressant medications.

Ruling Out Medications That Can Cause Depression

Narcotic pain medications, steroids, and antihypertensives are very different medications. But they share one thing in common. All three of these medication classes can cause depression or depression-like symptoms. And all three are common prescription medications.

Narcotic Pain Medications

The narcotic component in pain medications is what can cause depressive symptoms. There are many varieties of narcotics, and you should ask your doctor if you have any questions about depressive side effects. Not only can narcotics cause depression, they can also bring on confusion. This is especially true of meperidine (Demerol). These side effects are detrimental to recovery after a heart attack or open-heart surgery. The elderly and some others can be very sensitive to narcotics, and, therefore, when pain medication is prescribed, the person's mental state should be monitored. Different pain medications have different effects in the same individual. If one pain medication causes depression-like symptoms or confusion, ask your doctor whether the pain medicine is necessary, or request a change to another type of pain medication.

Steroids

Steroids such as prednisone can also occasionally cause depression. The stress hormone cortisol, secreted by the adrenal glands, is a steroid and is very similar to steroid medications. However, cortisol is lower in potency than prescription steroids. Many people take steroids for a host of conditions, from a skin rash to prevention of rejection after heart transplant. Some people describe a "high" or even manic symptoms when placed on a moderate to high dosage of steroids. When the steroid is later decreased or stopped, feelings of being "down" occur and depression may appear.

Antihypertensives

Older antihypertensive medications (that is, blood pressure medications) such as reserpine and methyldopa are well known to cause depression as a side effect. Beta-blockers, a very common heart medication, are used in treating coronary artery disease and rhythm disturbances as well as high blood pressure. In the past, it was felt that beta-blockers can cause depression, but recent research suggests that beta-blockers do not cause major depression. In the first thirty months of one study, although some patients complained of tiredness, slowness, and a "blah" mood when on a beta-blocker, no difference in the frequency of depressive symptoms was found between placebo and beta-blocker groups.

Treating Depression in Patients with Cardiovascular Disease

Depression in the setting of cardiovascular disease should be treated aggressively. This is because depression can adversely affect the person with heart disease in many ways. For example, depression can lead to poor compliance with medical therapy and self-care, and outcomes associated with cardiovascular disease are worsened in the presence of depression. The more severe the depression in a cardiac patient, the shorter the survival time appears to be, as opposed to mild to moderate depression, although even mild to moderate depression increases mortality in people with heart disease.

Antidepressant therapy can reduce depressive symptoms and improve the quality of life for people with heart disease who are suffering from depression. However, it is not yet known whether treatment of depression in those with heart disease actually increases survival rates. Close to four hundred people who had unstable angina or who had survived a heart attack were randomly treated with the antidepressant sertraline or a placebo (see SADHART study discussed below). While sertraline improved depression, especially in those with a history of major depression, no changes in the number of cardiac events or in the outcome were noted. Larger studies are needed to study this question more fully.

What about cognitive impairment such as poor memory and inability to concentrate—both of which can be either part of depression or made worse by depression? (Indeed, depression itself can cause a pseudodementia, which is sometimes referred to as the dementia of depression and is also a frequent component of Alzheimer's disease and other dementias.) Antidepressant therapy, therefore, is often initiated for individuals with cognitive impairment who also meet the criteria for major depression. Antidepressants can improve the memory and concentration, as well as the mood, of those with major depression and pseudodementia. In those who have fixed dementias, cognition is not likely to improve, though the depression can lift.

Antidepressant Medications for Heart Patients

For someone with heart disease and depression, are some antidepressants better than others? Are there any special precautions that one should take? Table 14.1 lists some of the more common antidepressants, and the sections that follow discuss their relative merits for heart patients.

**Table 14.1 Common Antidepressants by Type
(Including Generic and Brand Name)**

Type	Generic (Brand) Name
Tricyclic antidepressants	Amitriptyline (Elavil)
	Doxepin (Sinequan)
	Desipramine (Norpramin)
	Imipramine (Tofranil)
	Nortriptyline (Pamelor)
Selective serotonin reuptake inhibitors (SSRIs)	Citalopram (Celexa)
	Escitalopram (Lexapro)
	Fluoxetine (Prozac)
	Fluvoxamine (Luvox)
	Sertraline (Zoloft)
	Paroxetine (Paxil)
Serotonin-norepinephrine reuptake inhibitors	Duloxetine (Cymbalta)
	Venlafaxine (Effexor)
Norepinephrine and dopamine reuptake inhibitor	Bupropion (Wellbutrin/Zyban)
Serotonin autoreceptor antagonist and reuptake inhibitor	Nefazodone (Serzone)
	Trazodone (Desyrel)
Serotonin autoreceptor antagonist	Mirtazapine (Remeron)

Tricyclic Antidepressants

Before the development of selective serotonin reuptake inhibitors (SSRIs), the primary medications for patients with depression included a group of drugs called tricyclic antidepressants (TCAs). TCAs include medications such as imipramine, doxepin, amitriptyline, desipramine, and nortriptyline.

These medications have a side effect profile that is somewhat risky for patients with cardiac disease. TCAs can cause what is known as *orthostatic* or *postural hypotension*. This refers to the dysfunctional tendency for blood pressure to drop significantly when one goes from a prone position to a sitting position or from a sitting position to a standing position. This is particularly a problem in patients who have severe coronary artery disease and abnormal left heart functions.

TCAs also have numerous drug interactions and produce anti-cholinergic side effects such as dry mouth, constipation, urinary retention, and rapid heart rate. More important, they may cause electrical conduction abnormalities in the heart, which can lead to heart block.

As a group, TCAs are also known to be proarrhythmic—that is, prone to cause heart rhythm disturbances even though they are technically Type 1A antiarrhythmic drugs. This means they can lower the threshold for ventricular arrhythmias (heartbeat abnormalities), including lethal ones such as ventricular tachycardia and ventricular fibrillation. These are the same rhythm disturbances that most often cause sudden cardiac death.

The use of TCAs is discouraged in patients after a heart attack, particularly during the first two months—which is also a vulnerable period for the development of depression.

Selective Serotonin Reuptake Inhibitors (SSRIs)

SSRIs have become first-line drugs for depression, even among people without coronary artery disease. Escitalopram, citalopram, sertraline, fluoxetine, paroxetine, and fluvoxamine are all SSRIs. They are generally safe and are better tolerated by people with stable heart disease. There is some evidence, however, that citalopram can lower the threshold for ventricular arrhythmias, particularly when used with an antipsychotic medication called pimozide (Orap).

Research is being conducted to determine whether treatment of depression with antidepressants reduces the risk of coronary artery disease. To date, however, little substantive information is available on the benefit to heart patients of medications such as SSRIs. The Sertraline Antidepressant Heart Randomized Trial (SADHART), directed by Columbia psychiatrists Alexander Glassman and Peter Shapiro, was a multicentered, double-blind, randomized, controlled, large-scale study of the safety and efficacy of sertraline treatment in patients after a heart attack. The SADHART study showed that sertraline treatment was associated with clinical improvement in mood and was well tolerated in more than 85 percent of patients with major depression after a heart attack. A significant reduction in cardiac events on sertraline was not proved; however, sertraline was shown to be associated with reduced endothelium/platelet interaction and with improved quality of life in people who had suffered a heart attack. More studies are planned.

All in all, research on SSRIs and depression in heart patients is at a very early stage of development. The effectiveness of SSRIs in the treatment of depression is well documented. It remains to be seen in larger studies whether this class of antidepressants help prevent the development of coronary artery disease and reduce adverse outcomes after heart attacks and coronary bypass surgery among people who are depressed.

SSRI Drug Interactions

There has been some concern about potential interaction between SSRIs and other drugs. Interaction with warfarin (Coumadin), a potent blood thinner used by many heart patients, has received the most attention. The level of Coumadin in the blood can increase due to SSRI displacement of Coumadin from its binding sites on the protein albumin, and this can lead to a bleeding tendency. People on both SSRIs and warfarin should be followed closely by their doctors with more frequent prothrombin time (PT) and international normalized ratio (INR) blood tests.

SSRIs can inhibit the cytochrome P450 liver isoenzyme system, and this reduces the clearance of medications that are normally broken down by this liver enzyme system. This can lead to higher medication levels and side effects.

SSRIs should not be given to patients on class 1C antiarrhythmic agents such as encainide, mexiletine (Mexitil), and propafenone (Rythmol), because their levels may increase as well. Beta-blocking medications can also be enhanced by SSRIs, so caution must also be exercised with this combination.

"Serotonin Syndrome"

When high levels or mixed usage of serotonin-enhancing drugs are present, a serotonin syndrome, characterized by mental changes, agitation, restlessness, sweating, shivering, jerking movements, tremor, fever, rigidity, hyperactive reflexes, and autonomic nervous system dysfunction, may occur. Most often the culprits are a combination of an SSRI and a monoamine oxidase inhibitor (MAOI) or an MAOI and meperidine (Demerol). When a serotonin syndrome occurs, these medications must be stopped.

Other Side Effects of SSRIs

People taking SSRIs have had rare occurrences of rapid heart rhythm disturbance (tachyarrhythmia) and slow heart rhythm (bradyarrhythmia). Overall, the cardiac side effects of SSRIs appear to be extremely low. Other side effects include gastrointestinal upset, restlessness and insomnia, and sexual dysfunction. There is also some information to suggest that sertraline may have mild antiplatelet effects. Platelets, as you may recall, are blood components involved in clot formation.

Other Antidepressants

Venlafaxine is a serotonin-norepinephrine reuptake inhibitor (SNRI), which is effective for depression and anxiety. It may raise blood pressure, so this should be routinely checked when it is used. It can also cause dizziness. Duloxetine is another SNRI with the same effectiveness and similar side effects.

Treating Depression and Substance Abuse

Depressed patients often suffer from alcohol and/or substance abuse. Rehabilitation from alcohol and substance abuse should not distract from the recognition and treatment of depression, and the reverse also holds true. More than 60 percent of alcoholics are depressed when they come for a detoxification stay, and their depressed mood may persist during the early weeks of sobriety. Alcohol and substance abuse also increase suicide risk. Still, depression is not often diagnosable or treatable when someone is actively addicted to alcohol or other substances, so the first step is to detoxify and rehabilitate, and then if depression persists it can be aggressively treated.

Alcohol abuse can be screened for through the CAGE Questionnaire, published in the *American Journal of Psychiatry* by the American Psychiatric Association in 1974.

- Do you ever feel as though you need to cut down on your drinking?
- Do people annoy you when they criticize your drinking?
- Do you ever feel bad or guilty about your drinking?
- Do you ever have a drink first thing in the morning to steady your nerves or to get rid of a hangover (eye opener)?

If you answer yes to two or more of these questions, you likely have an alcohol problem in need of attention.

Another antidepressant that appears to be well tolerated in patients with cardiac disease is bupropion (Wellbutrin). A brand of bupropion, Zyban, is also used as an antismoking agent.

Antidepressants such as trazodone and nefazodone have side effects such as sedation and hypotension, which limit their use in people with heart disease. Nefazodone is rarely used these days because of potential liver damage. Mirtazapine can cause weight gain and sedation.

Depression accounts for approximately 60 percent of all suicides. Antidepressants are used to relieve depression and reduce suicide risk when it is part of the symptomatology. Nevertheless, all antidepressants can excite a depressed patient, and in so doing, suicidal thoughts and behaviors can worsen. Because of this risk, patients on antidepressants need to be closely monitored by their doctors for suicidality.

Nonpharmacological Treatment of Depression

Beside medications, several different kinds of therapy can be used to treat depression. The most reassuring way to choose among them is to select the therapy that seems to best fit your personal needs and situation. All these therapies are potentially valuable to a person who has coronary artery disease and mood dysfunction. The combination of antidepressants and therapies such as cognitive behavioral therapy has been shown to be particularly effective for depression.

Cognitive Behavioral Therapy

In cognitive behavioral therapy (CBT), you and your therapist form an active partnership to modify your negative emotions and behaviors stimulated by habitual situations. This is an effective treatment approach for both anxiety and depression in people with coronary artery disease. The same approach can also be used to help people modify cardiac risk factors such as social isolation. Cognitive behavioral therapy is made up of two components. The cognitive component focuses on identifying and reducing pessimistic or self-critical thinking that leads to depression. The behavioral component focuses on increasing the individual's participation in rewarding activities and reducing behaviors that reinforce depression. There are a limited number of sessions, usually ten to twelve, and homework is given.

In a recent eighteen-month study of 120 adults who had attempted suicide, CBT reduced self-reported depression and hopelessness and

Electroconvulsive Therapy (ECT)

Electroconvulsive therapy (ECT) is the most effective therapy for severe medication-resistant depression. ECT has important effects on the heart, including a very short-term alteration of heart rate and impairment of heart function. ECT can infrequently provoke significant electrocardiographic abnormalities. Even though there are isolated reports of cardiac fatalities with ECT, its safety record in patients with cardiac disease is actually quite good.

ECT provokes a sympathetic nervous system burst, resulting in temporary high blood pressure and rapid heart rate. However, these cardiovascular effects can be reduced through the use of alpha-blockers and beta-blockers, which dampen sympathetic nervous system overactivity during the procedure that is performed with the assistance of an anesthesiologist. This precaution has reduced the incidence of serious cardiac complications. ECT probably should be avoided in people with severe coronary artery disease, manifested as unstable angina. People in the midst of a heart attack also should not undergo ECT therapy. Aside from these two groups, most experts believe that ECT is quite safe and effective for severely depressed individuals with long-term heart disease.

was significantly better than usual care in preventing future suicide attempts.

Interpersonal Therapy

Interpersonal therapy is more what people generally think of as psychotherapy. This form of therapy seeks to clarify and work out interpersonal issues such as role disputes, social isolation, role transition, or prolonged grief responses. The goal is to aid you in forming interpersonal relationships that help you satisfy emotional and behavioral needs, instead of maintaining negative emotions.

Problem-Solving Therapy

Problem-solving therapy helps you identify and settle current life challenges. This may involve breaking up larger difficulties into smaller ones that are more manageable. Resolving a major crisis in a step-by-step approach is a more effective way for many people to achieve positive changes.

Emotional Support

One of the main therapeutic interventions that can be provided to someone with cardiac disease is emotional support. This intervention can be provided by your family members and friends. The importance of emotional support should not be underestimated. Emotional support may take root in the strengthening of family ties or in a caring doctor-patient relationship. The goal is for you to achieve solace in the expansion and deepening of a social support network.

In the next chapter, we provide further strategies to help you manage stress and work toward continuous cardiovascular health.

15

A Healthy Heart
Takes a Healthy Mind

THERE ARE MANY STEPS that you can take to keep your cardiovascular health in optimal shape. Good nutrition, exercise, weight control, and avoidance of smoking are all important, and materials about these topics are available at many sources. In this chapter, however, we look at several additional steps that are important to your cardiovascular health, including how to stay informed about advances in cardiovascular and mental health.

Managing Stress

Turning to the individual, what is the best way to control stress? In his excellent book *Conquering Heart Disease: New Ways to Live Well Without Drugs or Surgery*, Dr. Harvey B. Simon of Massachusetts General Hospital suggests that people use an emotional self-assessment test to gauge the cardiac risk associated with their emotional state. He reminds readers to review answers with their spouses, relatives, or friends to make sure that they are being objective; and he recommends that stress control should be a part of any program to fight atherosclerotic disease.

Behavioral Exercises

Dr. Simon also talks about behavioral exercises and remarks that behavioral patterns like type A behavior can be changed through certain exercises. These are some examples:

- Drive your car in the slow lane, and use your car horn only to avert accidents, not to vent frustration and anger.
- When you drive up to a toll plaza, join the longest line, even if you have exact change.
- Put your cart in the longest supermarket checkout lane, even if your basket qualifies for the express lane.
- Eat slowly, trying to be the last person to finish the meal.
- Talk slowly and don't interrupt.
- Don't put in the last word in an argument, even if you are sure you're right.
- Keep your voice down; never shout.
- Don't use expletives. Find less hostile substitutes.
- Don't permit yourself outbursts of anger. Instead, wait a few moments, take some deep breaths, and express yourself calmly.
- Leave early for plays and concerts so that you don't have to rush. Plan to spend ten minutes relaxing in your seat before the curtain goes up.
- Don't do two things at once. For example, hang up the phone before opening your mail or emptying the dishwasher.
- Don't set your alarm clock on weekends.
- Don't set your watch ahead. Even better, don't look at your watch more than once an hour. Best of all, don't wear your watch on weekends.
- Don't plan all your time. Start by leaving an evening free, then a day, and then a weekend.

Relaxation Exercises

Relaxation techniques can help to reduce stress. They teach you to use your mind to relax your body. Mental stress produces physical signs and symptoms such as these:

- Tense muscles
- Restlessness
- Tension headaches
- Low-back pain
- Dry mouth
- Swallowing difficulty with a lump in the throat
- Jaw clenching
- Bruxism (grinding your teeth)
- Stomach cramps, heartburn, or diarrhea
- Rapid heartbeat
- Chest tightness
- Rapid breathing or sighing
- Repeated coughing

Relaxation techniques can help reduce these symptoms of stress.

In his pioneering book *The Relaxation Response*, Dr. Herbert Benson of the Mind Body Medical Institute at the Beth Israel Deaconess Medical Center in Boston says that a key ingredient in any relaxation technique is breaking the train of everyday thought. In the relaxation response, you spend five to ten minutes in a quiet place, and start out by taking deep cleansing breaths. You slowly push out your stomach so that the diaphragm expands maximally, hold the breath briefly, and then exhale slowly. You can choose a focus that can be religious (such as a statement or an image of spiritual significance) or a secular symbol of solace and support (such as the face of a loved one or an important saying). The deep-breathing sequences should be repeated ten to twenty times. This relaxation response can be achieved at any time during the day, though it should be done at least once or twice a day. There are multiple ways to achieve the relaxation response, such as through prayer, yoga, meditation, and tai chi. All are characterized by the breaking of the train of everyday thought and by repetition or repetitive behavior. The Mind-Body Medical Institute has shown over the years that learning the relaxation response combined with group cognitive behavioral therapy can help relieve stress-related illnesses like hypertension, angina, asthma, insomnia, and headache and help with disorders such as infertility.

Another way to relax is through progressive muscle relaxation, sometimes called the Jacobsen relaxation technique. This focuses on each major muscle group in sequence, with a tightening and mainte-nance of the contraction for twenty seconds, followed by a releasing of the tension. As the muscle relaxes, you are urged to concentrate on the release of the tension and the sensation of relaxation. You are asked to start with the face and then move down the body—from forehead to eyes to tongue to cheeks to jaws to neck to back to chest to stom-ach to buttocks and thighs to arms and forearms and hands to calves and ankles and feet. This sequence of muscular relaxation takes about twelve to fifteen minutes and is suggested twice a day.

Biofeedback

Biofeedback is an autoregulation stress-reducing technique. When undergoing biofeedback, you are linked to electrical monitors. These monitors measure your blood pressure, pulse, respiratory rate, muscle tension, and skin temperature. Audiovisual devices inform you of phys-iological improvements as you relax. This reinforces stress-reducing mental actions that result in the triggering of the audiovisual devices. Biofeedback is not as convenient as the other techniques and requires specialized facilities and a skilled practitioner.

Yoga and Other Physical Activities

Yoga is another way to relax muscles and the mind. It can be used as a form of muscle-relaxation technique and can be combined with med-itation. Meditation can also be grafted onto the relaxation response. It has now been shown that meditation techniques increase heart rate variability (a positive response), and this may have important implica-tions for why meditation might be helpful in those at risk for or suf-fering from cardiovascular diseases. Rhythmic chanting can slow the respiratory rate.

In addition, all physical exercise is very good for reducing stress. Aerobic exercise especially has the ability to improve spirits, counter depression, and dissipate stress.

Self-Regulating Life Stress

No one today can avoid stress. Of course, it is unlikely that anyone in human history has ever been able to avoid it. But there are ways to reduce the harmful effects of stress in our lives. As Dr. Simon points out, you should start by identifying your sources of stress, and then try to restructure your lifestyle to meet these sources of stress head-on. You can go on to break through denial of tension, express your concerns and stressors to supportive individuals, and recognize that thinking positively is healthier than sustaining negative emotions. You can also develop good habits that help you embrace "good stress" activities like exercise, listening to music, getting enough sleep, not overusing alcohol, and refraining from all use of nicotine and recreational drugs. Of key importance are improving interpersonal skills and building a network of social support to avoid social isolation. Getting help for emotional distress is also essential. If you can build a balanced life filled with work and play and exercise and rest—all the while balancing your own needs with those of your family and community—you stand a very good chance of staying healthy and happy, despite the stress of present-day society.

The Role of Spirituality in Health

It is always important to maintain meaningfulness at all stages of your life. This often brings up a discussion of religion and spirituality and their effects on health. In fact, an association between religious behavior and better health, including improved cardiovascular health, appears to exist. The association in some studies is mild, while in others it is moderate, but it does appear to be valid. Whether the association is causal or not is still open to debate and further research. Much more methodologically sound research will be needed to answer the causality question. Nevertheless, one recent study looked at 151 older patients who underwent coronary bypass surgery.

The result showed that most patients prayed about their post-operative problems and that private prayer appeared to significantly decrease depression and general distress one year after the bypass surgery. If you assume that reducing depressive mood can benefit cardiac outcome—and, as we have seen, this is by no means a clear-cut assumption at this point—private prayer may in the future be shown to have some effect in reducing risk of future cardiac events. For example, if you feel that anger is one of your cardiac risk factors, changing your behavior patterns through the ways mentioned earlier and becoming more spiritual and loving in your focus may lessen your hostility.

Lessening of hostility through forgiveness is another way in which religion has a role in improving health outcomes. In a study, college students and their middle-aged parents, all of whom had undergone a deep family hurt, had their health measured according to two physical health indexes. One index listed reported ailments; the other listed physician-diagnosed illnesses. The researchers also measured hostility levels using a standard hostility index. In both students and their parents, the least-forgiving individuals had more physical problems, both on self-report and on physician diagnosis. The researchers then looked at which was a better predictor of heart disease: lack of forgiveness or hostility. Lack of forgiveness turned out to be the better predictor.

In another study on forgiveness, researchers looked at survey responses for more than fourteen hundred adults during a five-month period. Among their findings was the fact that young adults (aged eighteen to forty-four) were less likely to forgive others than middle-aged (aged forty-five to sixty-four) and older (aged sixty-five and older) adults. The young adults were also less likely to believe that they had been forgiven by God. Among all the participants of all ages, forgiveness of themselves and others was associated with decreased psychological distress and decreased feelings of restlessness, hopelessness, and nervousness. Satisfaction was also higher in those who reported high levels of forgiveness.

The Stanford Forgiveness Project teaches seven steps to forgiveness:

1. The first step is to figure out how you feel during the traumatic moment that leads to the separation between two people.
2. The second step is to acknowledge that forgiveness is for your own healing and is important for you as well as for the one forgiven.
3. The third step is to begin the process right away. You need to remind yourself of the good things in your life. When you are feeling upset, deep breathing and the relaxation response can be practiced, which can create a receptivity to forgive.
4. The fourth step is to change your expectations. Don't expect things to go your way all the time, and be appreciative when they do.
5. The fifth step is to find your own positive intention. Discover what it was that you wished for but didn't get from the person that disappointed you. This could be love, friendship, validation, or something else.
6. The sixth step is to find a new way to achieve your positive intention.
7. The seventh step is to be in your story by telling it in a way that reflects your positive intention. It will become a story of how you were disappointed and hurt but managed to move forward with optimism in your life.

The John Templeton Foundation, which is interested in the interrelationship of science, medicine, and religion, has funded research into the effects of forgiveness on health. Incidentally, the foundation has also begun to fund research on the effects of altruistic behavior on health.

Staying Informed About Heart Disease and Mental Health

One of the best ways to keep yourself healthy is to stay informed about coronary artery disease and mental health. Today, there are many sources for excellent information. The challenge is in knowing where to look and how to differentiate good information from bad information. Your doctor can usually provide some basic, solid information, but you may wish to supplement what you have been told. This effort depends entirely on your initiative.

Most available lay information is currently segregated into either heart disease or mental health topics. There is very little information on the interrelationships between these two conditions. This book is one of the first major publications that focuses on this interesting area.

If you need information on heart disease, mental health, or any other health topics, the doctor's office and hospital are good places to start. A variety of printed materials and audiovisual tapes are frequently available. In many hospitals, designated health educators are on staff for patients and their families. The local library is another good place for health information, and the librarian is a resource person that you should seek out for assistance. Today, the Internet can provide the most up-to-date and comprehensive information for anyone who has access to a computer. If you don't have computer access at home, the local library usually has computers for the public, and the librarian is frequently available to help with this search.

However, a major problem with the Internet is too much information, which itself can be a form of stress. It is also difficult to sort out what is accurate, reliable information.

For general information relating to heart disease, the American Heart Association has one of the best sites. The Internet address is www.americanheart.org.

Another choice is the site sponsored by the American College of Cardiology. While it is primarily for health professionals, consumer health information relating to heart disease is also available on the site. The Internet address is www.acc.org.

For information with a greater emphasis on heart surgery, there are several choices. The Society of Thoracic Surgeons has an excellent website. The Internet address is www.sts.org.

The federal government has several excellent websites for health information. At the National Library of Medicine, there are two choices. Medline, primarily for professionals, provides abstracts of scientific publications. It requires skills in how to do a medical search and may be too complex for the typical consumer. The whole article can be ordered from the National Library of Medicine or, in some cases, directly from the publishers. Because there are usually many articles on a specific topic and it is difficult to determine the quality of each report, it is appropriate only for those undertaking a serious research project. The National Library of Medicine also has Medlineplus, a site that provides health information for the public. The Internet address for these two sources is www.nlm.nih.gov.

For information relating to heart disease, the federal government has two other excellent sites: the National Heart, Lung, and Blood Institute and the Agency for Health Care Policy and Research. In addition to information on their sites, printed materials are available. Their Internet addresses are www.nhlbi.nih.gov and www.ahcpr.gov.

The federal government also provides excellent information relating to mental health through the National Institute of Mental Health and the Agency for Health Care Policy and Research. Their Internet addresses are www.nimh.nih.gov and www.ahcpr.gov.

A website very useful to people with any illness or disability is Disability Resources. It provides information for the consumer on specific illnesses and disabilities, available resources arranged by state and subdivided by topic, Internet resources arranged by specific conditions, and a host of other resources. The Internet address is www.disability resources.org.

For more online resources for finding help and information on general and specific mental health conditions, depression, anger, anxiety, and panic disorders, as well as women's issues, look through the Selected References at the end of this book.

PART IV

Special Considerations for Women

16

Women's Hearts

Jean, seventy-two, lived in Wilmette, Illinois, a suburb north of Chicago. She had diabetes, for which she took two different pills. Having smoked a pack of cigarettes a day for twenty-five years, she no longer smoked. Her husband had died several years earlier, but she maintained a close relationship with her four children and her circle of friends. The first sign of her coronary artery disease was an intermittent burning discomfort in her chest. She initially didn't make much of it, and neither did her family doctor. When this symptom persisted for four months, she was referred to a cardiologist for further evaluation. A stress test confirmed that she had coronary artery disease, and the cardiologist prescribed several pills for her condition.

Jean did well for about eight months, and then her chest pain returned. After another positive stress test, she underwent an angiogram, which showed three major blockages in her coronary arteries. Balloon angioplasty and stent placement gave her another year of relief. She underwent a second angiogram, which showed more blockages but a strong heart. Surgery was recommended, and Jean agreed to it after discussions with her children. She went through a triple coronary artery bypass without any problems, but three days later, she came down with pneumonia that required she be placed on a respirator. After a four-week stay in the intensive care unit, Jean was ready to move on with her rehabilitation from surgery, but she spent the entire day in her hospital bed. She barely communicated with anyone and refused to sit on a chair or exercise with the physical therapist. Jean told a nurse that she had had enough and wanted nature to take its course. She died two days later.

One of this chapter's most important messages is this: women and men are equally affected by coronary artery disease (the buildup of plaque in arteries on the heart's surface). However, coronary artery disease in women is frequently more severe than in men, women recover more slowly than men do, and they are more likely to die from heart attacks and cardiac surgery. Depression, a condition that women are more prone to, may play an important contributory role. Coronary artery disease is a preventable condition, and this chapter can help you take the necessary steps to protect yourself.

For a number of reasons, a major one being that for a very long time heart disease in women wasn't being addressed as seriously as it was for men, women have not paid sufficient attention to coronary artery disease. The condition affects many women as they enter into menopause. Angina, heart attack, angioplasty, and bypass surgery can be both debilitating and life threatening. You have heard over and over again what preventive measures you need to take, but do not forget to also consider your emotions. We now know that negative feelings can promote coronary artery disease or make the preexisting heart disease worse. Understanding how and why depression, anxiety, and loneliness affect your cardiac health can make all the difference. If you develop depression, make sure you get the proper treatment.

Heart Disease: The Number One Killer of American Women

A woman's heart doesn't differ from a man's in its design and how it functions. The only difference is smaller coronary arteries in some women. Yet women often have very different experiences with cardiac problems, due to physical differences, emotional differences, and the way some doctors treat women with heart disease.

According to the American Heart Association and the American Cancer Society, 40,000 American women die each year from breast cancer and 250,000 American women die each year from coronary artery disease. However, most women worry far more about breast cancer than about heart disease. Many women continue to think of heart disease as a greater threat to men than to themselves. Yet heart disease, particularly in the form of coronary artery disease and stroke, is the number one killer of American women. The same is true for women in most developed countries. One in two women die of heart disease or stroke, compared with one in twenty-five who die of breast cancer.

A 1995 Gallup poll showed that four out of five American women were unaware that heart disease was the leading cause of death for women. More surprisingly, the poll showed that many physicians were also unaware of that fact. Even today, many women are puzzled when told they have coronary artery disease and need coronary bypass surgery.

Much has been made of the declining number of deaths due to cardiovascular disease in the United States over the past decade. More effective hospital care, lower smoking rates, and improvements in treatment of heart attacks have been credited for this decline, but this drop in the cardiovascular death rate tells only half the story. The much publicized drop is the combined rate for men and women together, and the decline in the number of deaths from heart disease has been far greater for men than for women. That a significant number of American women are dying from coronary artery disease is due in part to the increase in the number of aging women in the population and their cardiac risk factors.

Women's Risk Factors

The risk factors and preventive measures for coronary artery disease are different for men and women, according to research. This section shares some important points pertaining to risk factors in women.

During the last fifty years, change in social values has made it more acceptable for women to smoke. Accordingly, more women are smoking and, at the same time, fewer women than men have quit smoking. Some women have switched to low-tar and low-nicotine cigarettes under the misconception that these products are less harmful, but most are unaware that these cigarettes do not lower the risk of heart disease.

Studies show that lowering blood cholesterol benefits both men and women. However, these studies have included few women, so further research is necessary to explore the effects of estrogen and to confirm that the study results are true for women as well as men.

Among women, diabetes is common and more of a serious risk factor than it is in men. Among people with diabetes, death rates from coronary artery disease are three to seven times higher for women than for men.

Systolic high blood pressure is more common in older women than men. Studies have linked systolic high blood pressure to stroke and coronary artery disease in women.

Several studies have shown an increasing incidence of obesity in U.S. women. The Nurse Health Study evaluated 120,000 middle-aged women and found that obesity increased almost 40 percent over fourteen years. Currently, nearly 50 percent of American women are overweight, and 25 percent are obese. In one study, obesity increased the risk of coronary artery disease twofold. In addition, 40 percent of American women have a sedentary lifestyle, which has been linked to a higher risk of coronary artery disease.

Age also has a more profound impact on coronary artery disease in women than in men. Prior to menopause, estrogen helps protect women against coronary artery disease. After menopause, the risk of coronary artery disease in women gradually increases to a level equal to that of men. Up to the age of sixty, only one in seventeen American women has had a coronary event (heart attack or cardiac death), compared to one in five American men. However, after sixty, the number is the same: one in four American women and men die of coronary artery disease.

Another distinguishing risk factor for women involved the early forms of oral contraceptives that contained high doses of hormones. These pills have been linked to an increase in heart attacks, especially among women who smoked while taking them. However, the increased heart disease risk was eliminated after discontinuation of these contraceptives. The low-dose oral contraceptives used today are associated with significantly less risk of heart disease.

Chest Pain in Women

Many women suffer chest pain but are less frequently evaluated for coronary artery disease than men with the same symptom.

How likely is a woman's chest pain to be caused by the heart? Is her chest pain the same kind of symptom as a man's? To find out, British researchers analyzed data on all the women with chest pain referred to one cardiologist from 1987 to 1991. All the women subsequently had an arteriogram (an imaging test to reveal any blockages). The researchers followed up the health of these women for several years. Their findings can be summarized as follows:

- Chest pain in women is common.
- Other causes of chest pain are more common in women than men.
- Exercise stress testing and coronary angiogram accurately identify women with coronary artery disease.
- A woman may find that her chest pain is not caused by her heart, but, unfortunately, that explanation does not relieve her discomfort. Many women continue taking antiangina medications, although they know that their coronary arteries are normal.

In addition, women with chronic stable angina are more likely than men to suffer chest pain while resting, sleeping, or undergoing mental stress. Therefore, chest pain in women may have different clinical implications. Coronary artery disease in women usually first appears as angina; in men the first symptom is usually a heart attack. So chest pain in women must be evaluated as aggressively as in men. If you are a woman with chest pain, you should undergo a stress test and, if necessary, a coronary angiogram (an imaging test to reveal blockages in the coronary arteries).

When women are diagnosed with coronary artery disease, they should receive the same treatment that men are given. When coronary artery disease is not the cause of a woman's chest pain, physicians should seek and treat the other causes accordingly.

Women's Coronary Artery Disease

More research has been done on coronary artery disease than any other form of cardiovascular disease. For that reason, coronary artery disease is the kind of heart trouble that we pay most attention to in this book. Women generally develop coronary artery disease ten years later in age than men do, but once they develop the condition, women don't enjoy any survival advantage. In fact, women are more likely to die from a heart attack, balloon angioplasty, or coronary bypass surgery than men are.

In the Cardiovascular Health Study, the heart attack rate was 9.7 percent for women aged sixty-five to sixty-nine and 17.9 percent for women eighty-five and older. In addition, the following facts were emphasized in the report:

- After menopause, a woman has a 31 percent lifetime risk of death from coronary artery disease, in contrast to a 3 percent death risk from breast cancer or hip fracture.
- Of women forty-five to sixty-five years old, one in eight show signs of coronary artery disease.
- Of women over sixty-five years old, one in three show signs of coronary artery disease.
- Of people in the hospital due to a heart attack, 16 percent of the women die, as opposed to 11 percent of the men.
- A year after a heart attack, women's mortality rate is higher than the men's rate.

These findings confirm the seriousness of coronary artery disease among women. Because American women tend to have many coronary risk factors, most women can substantially benefit from preventive strategies. But women have frequently been excluded from coronary

Ethnic Differences Among Women

Coronary artery disease is more common among some ethnic groups than it is in others. Based on information from the American Heart Association, coronary artery disease is most prevalent among African-American women and least common in Asian-American women.

The situation is more complex for Latinas. Research has been conducted on Latinas from many diverse communities, and the data don't always agree. Overall, the rates of coronary artery disease in women look like this:

- African-American women have the highest rate.
- Latina and Caucasian women have similar rates, and they are about halfway between African-Americans and Asian-Americans.
- Asian-American women have the lowest rates.

These ethnic differences are a reflection of different risk factors, including family history and diet, access to medical care, and death from other causes.

artery disease studies or investigated only in small numbers. This lack of research makes it difficult for doctors to know which treatments are applicable to both women and men and which are applicable to one but not the other.

When a new cardiac drug comes into use based on clinical tests conducted mostly on men, can doctors assume that the medication has the same benefits and side effects in women? After all, women have a different hormonal composition, and their drug metabolism can be different. The answer is not always clear. But what can oversight agencies do? Refuse women a new drug that could possibly greatly benefit them? This whole area of medicine is fertile ground for further research.

Important Treatment Differences Between Men and Women

Men and women experience chest pain and heart disease differently, but the story doesn't end there. Some disturbing evidence shows inequality in the medical care that men and women receive. In addition, men and women don't respond to medical treatment in the same way. The following list sums up the most important physical and emotional differences between men and women who suffer from coronary artery disease:

- More women than men die from bypass surgery.
- Bypass surgery provides fewer benefits for women than it does for men.
- Women are more likely than men to suffer disabilities from their coronary artery disease symptoms.
- Women are more likely to experience mood disturbances after a heart attack.
- Women suffer cardiac, psychosomatic, and psychological symptoms more often than men do.
- Depression and anxiety are more likely to interfere with a woman's recovery than a man's.

Do Female Heart Attack Victims Receive the Same Treatment as Men Receive?

Researchers investigated whether women having heart attacks received the same treatment as their male counterparts in the university and city hospitals of Nottingham, in the English Midlands. They concluded that female heart attack victims' chances of survival were reduced because their treatment was not as good as the treatment provided for men— both in the hospital and after discharge. Here is a summary of the researchers' findings:

- Female heart attack victims took longer to arrive at the hospital than their male counterparts did.
- Women were less likely than men to be admitted to the coronary care unit and less likely to receive clot-dissolving treatment.

- Women's heart attacks were generally more serious than the men's were.
- Women had a higher death rate than men on admission to the hospital.
- On discharge from the hospital, women were less likely than men to be on a regimen of heart medications, such as beta-blockers.

It could be argued, of course, that in this case what is true for England is not necessarily true for the United States. However, researchers in New York demonstrated similar findings. They found that women were significantly less likely than men to undergo a balloon angioplasty (to reestablish blood flow to oxygen-starved heart muscles) within six hours of a heart attack.

Balloon Angioplasty for Women Who've Had a Heart Attack

In the New York study described in the previous section, the women undergoing balloon angioplasty after a heart attack were older and more likely to have advanced coronary artery disease, high blood pressure, diabetes, buildup of plaque elsewhere in the body (other than the heart), and cardiac instability resulting from their heart attacks. Not surprisingly, the death rate for women in that study was nearly 8 percent, compared to 2.5 percent for men. Even after adjusting for age, the women still had a higher death rate. In fact, the study observed a higher death rate among the younger women.

Even though that study focused on women who underwent balloon angioplasty after a heart attack, other studies have reported similar findings on women's outcomes after a heart attack.

Balloon Angioplasty for Women Who Haven't Had a Heart Attack

What about balloon angioplasty not in the setting of a heart attack? Overall, both women and men have comparably high success rates for angioplasty. However, relief of angina symptoms and long-term survival are poorer in women. This difference can be attributed to greater age, smaller vessels, and more extensive disease among women. Women appear to have slightly more procedure-related complications, such as bleeding, injury in the groin vessel where the catheter is introduced, and injury in the coronary artery. The fact that most women have smaller vessels than men may be the cause.

Coronary Bypass Surgery for Women

Women generally have bypass surgery at a more advanced age than men do. By the time women have the surgery, they have greater functional impairment and are more likely to have severe and unstable angina—so the surgery is usually urgent or even an emergency. Women are twice as likely as men to die during bypass surgery. Women's smaller size, smaller coronary arteries, and more advanced age increase the difficulty of coronary bypass surgery and contribute to a generally higher death rate. The bypasses constructed from leg veins work less well in women.

The Myth of Female Protection

The most striking difference between women and men in cardiovascular health is called *female protection*. This term is misleading, because it suggests that women are not subject to the same cardiac risks that men are. *Delay* would be a more accurate word than *protection*. Women have most of the same cardiovascular risks that men have—only ten years later.

This delay is a benefit to women. One major drawback, however, is that when a woman first develops a heart condition, she is likely to be a decade older than her male counterpart—which means that her powers of recovery are weaker. Greater age, finer and more delicate blood vessels, and less physical robustness are thought to cause the poorer recovery rates that women have from heart attacks and cardiac surgery in comparison to men. Emotional causes, such as depression, are more likely to combine with these physical causes for heart disease in women.

In addition, women are less likely than men to obtain relief from their symptoms in having a bypass operation, they more often have subsequent cardiac events, and they are more likely to require further surgery within five years.

In a large, multi-institutional study of 416,347 patients undergoing cardiac surgery (32 percent women), women had a higher risk of postoperative complications of the brain. They also had a higher death rate within a month of developing these complications.

The Good News and the Bad News

The previous sections have offered discouraging news for the female patient who needs balloon angioplasty or bypass surgery, but some recent reports have also shown that coronary bypass outcomes for women have improved and are equivalent to men. Contributing factors to this improvement include a better selection of patients for surgery, progress in surgical techniques, and improvement in the care of patients after surgery.

Ten Ways for Women to Prevent Coronary Artery Disease

Coronary artery disease develops slowly, often over many years. Therefore, a woman needs to think about prevention *before* menopause, when she will lose the cardiac protection from estrogen that protects her heart. Four misconceptions may interfere with her taking measures to enhance the future health of her heart.

- It is more important to worry about breast cancer.
- Men, not women, have heart trouble.
- It'll never happen to me.
- I don't have time right now.

All of these ideas are wrong and can be deadly.

Compelling evidence shows that coronary artery disease is largely a preventable illness. A committee of American physicians, nurses, and dietitians, chaired by Dr. Lori Mosca of New York Presbyterian Hospital, published a guide for risk reduction for women. This guide is approved by the American Heart Association and the American College of Cardiology. The following ten guidelines are based on that guide.

These guidelines are for reasonably healthy people. If you already have a heart condition or another illness, discuss these guidelines with your physician before following them.

1. Stop smoking. It's also a good idea to avoid secondhand cigarette smoke.
2. Exercise about a half hour each day. You can build this half hour in small increments throughout the day.
3. Cut back on saturated fat, sugar, and salt. Eat fresh vegetables and fruits at least twice a day, preferably five or more servings. Choose high-fiber foods.
4. Lose weight, if you're overweight. Try eating a bit less and exercising a bit more. If you need help, join a weight-loss group and/or gym.
5. Stay in touch with family and friends, manage stress effectively, and make an effort to improve your quality of life.
6. Have your blood pressure checked. If it's above normal, listen to your doctor's advice.
7. Have your cholesterol level checked. If it's too high, try to lower it through diet and exercise. Learn about and consider the different kinds of cholesterol-lowering medications.
8. Have your fasting blood sugar level checked for signs of diabetes.
9. If you take oral contraceptives, take the lowest effective dosage.
10. Consult with your physician if you are considering hormone replacement therapy.

In the next chapter, we look at how women and men compare in emotional risks.

17

The Effects of
Stress and Depression
on Women's Hearts

WOMEN ARE MORE LIKELY than men to receive treatment for an emotional condition, but they are less likely to receive treatment for a heart condition. Therefore, in this chapter, we focus on how women and men differ in their emotions and the cardiac consequences of those differences.

Much of this chapter is rooted in our clinical experiences and our speculations, because the medical world knows little about the interplay of emotions, gender, and coronary artery disease. Although many studies focus on the cardiac effects of various negative emotions, most have been done on men, even though more women than men suffer from these emotional disorders. Even when women are included in studies, their numbers are often too small to enable significant statistical conclusions to be drawn.

How Men and Women Respond
to Life Stresses

We have known for a long time that women are twice as likely as men to develop depression. Additionally, adult women are two to three times more likely than adult men to suffer from dysthymic disorder, which is a chronically depressed mood that lasts most of the day on more days than not for at least two years. That depression is often a response to stressful life events is also well established, so we make the connection that women respond differently to stressful life events.

Women tend to differ from men in what they find stressful. Researchers interviewed participants about eighteen different kinds of stressful life events and the onset of major depression. Women and men consistently reported being most distressed by different kinds of events. The researchers found that divorce or separation and work problems were major causes of depression in men, whereas interpersonal relationship problems were the major cause in women. However, they found no evidence that women encountered more stresses than men or were more sensitive to stress.

There is also the possibility that more women have an altered immune system that may make them vulnerable to depression. It has long been known that women outnumber men in terms of autoimmune diseases. Postpartum depression may be a version of this with reduction in serotonin precursor stores occurring when macrophage tryptophan production is reduced during pregnancy.

Emotional and Stress Links to Heart Disease in Women

Studies suggest that women are emotionally different from men, and those differences have a direct impact on women's hearts and their responses to heart disease. Here, we outline a few general features that are relevant to heart disease, and we explore some of these concepts in more depth in the following sections.

- Women are more inclined than men to express their emotions intensely in words.
- Women are more likely to develop a strong social network and depend on an intimate personal relationship.
- Life events and stresses tend to affect men and women differently.
- Men tend to feel anger more frequently than women do.
- Men express their emotions with higher levels of physiological arousal than women do.

- Alcoholism is more common in men, while eating disorders are more prevalent in women.
- Menopause can be associated with profound emotional fluctuations, including depression.
- Attempted suicides are more common in women, while completed suicides are more common in men.

Many of these emotional differences between females and males remain true even across cultural lines. In addition, studies on animals have shown that females housed alone manifested more anxiety and depression, while males tend to demonstrate the exact opposite trait.

Depression

In Chapter 4, we looked at how depression is linked to coronary artery disease and cardiac events, such as heart attack and sudden cardiac death. With depression twice as common in women, what are its effects on women's heart disease?

A ten-year study of five thousand women and nearly three thousand men who were free of coronary artery disease at the beginning of the project found that depression was a risk factor for coronary artery disease in both men and women. While depression was associated with more cardiac deaths in men, this was not the case in women. This excellent study is important because it showed that depression increased coronary artery disease in women as in men.

What is puzzling is why depression did not increase heart disease mortality among the women. The findings of the study are credible because the study design was good, the number of participants was large, and the duration of the study was long. Others studies offer the same data. Overall, these studies suggest that even though depression is twice as prevalent in women, it is not as strong a risk factor for coronary artery disease severity in women as in men.

Social and Economic Status

The health of 9,351 women—aged twenty-eight to fifty-five years, who visited the department of preventive medicine at a Swedish hospital—was followed for almost eleven years. The women who suffered cardiac events were likely to have a number of the following six characteristics.

- Have a smoking history
- Have high blood pressure
- Have a high cholesterol level
- Have a prediabetic or diabetic condition
- Have a low-paying job
- Have a lower educational level

While low socioeconomic status is linked to coronary artery disease in both women and men, its influence on women is stronger. Dutch psychologists cited an analysis of mortality trends of women under sixty-five years old in England and Wales over a period of forty years. Women in the lowest social class were one and a half times more likely to die of coronary artery disease than women of the highest class. Women married to men with unskilled jobs had a still higher death rate from coronary artery disease than their husbands had. In fact, American women with less than eight years of education had almost four times the risk of developing coronary artery disease than women with more than twelve years of education.

It is also worth noting that women of low socioeconomic and educational levels often have coronary-prone lifestyle patterns. Heavy smoking, high stress levels, diets with foods rich in sugar or saturated fat, and little physical exercise are typical of their lifestyle. Such women are often angry, pessimistic, depressed, and dissatisfied with their jobs. They usually have low self-esteem and little social support. The interaction of stress and lifestyle is likely to increase vulnerability to the metabolic syndrome described in an earlier chapter.

Employment

Work can have a profound effect on your emotional well-being. The employed are generally healthier than the unemployed—in both women and men. In the San Antonio Heart Study, 576 employed women were compared to 465 full-time homemakers. The only difference found between the two groups was that employed women had significantly higher levels of HDL (good cholesterol), which had a protective effect on their hearts. This was found to be due to their eating a healthier diet, smoking less, and exercising more than the homemakers. The protective effects of employment against heart disease appeared to be greater for women in professional and managerial careers than women in blue-collar jobs.

Working women with children are in a different situation. They have the increased workload of job and home. In addition to anger and frustration, such women may feel a lack of control over their lives and a feeling of being pulled from their different responsibilities. In a Swedish study of about four hundred thousand working women and six hundred thousand working men, women more frequently complained of headaches and fatigue than men did. Women who regularly worked overtime also had an increased risk of nonfatal heart attacks.

Tensions between career and family commitment were examined as a risk factor for coronary artery disease in 2,020 professional women between fifty and seventy years old. A significantly higher rate of coronary artery disease occurred in women who felt that their husband and children had held them back in their careers. This was true also for women who felt they had hurt their families through their career ambitions.

It seems that employment may provide some protection against heart disease for women, but trying to balance the demands of a job and family at the same time can involve cardiac risk. This, of course, may not be news to many women in these circumstances.

Social Network and Support

Social support and community ties appear to be equally important to cardiac health in women and men. The Stockholm Female Coronary Risk Study included 131 women, aged thirty to sixty-five years, who were hospitalized for an acute coronary event. The researchers reported that women with little social support were two and a half times more likely to have serious coronary artery disease than women with strong social support.

In addition, many studies have reported an increased risk of death in both men and women due to all causes in the months after the death of their spouse. While some studies claim that women have a greater risk than men, others have found the opposite. Both women and men have been reported to have an increased risk of coronary artery disease after the death of a spouse. Grief and emotional distress may predispose people to arrhythmias leading to cardiac mortality in the period immediately after the death of a spouse.

How Women Respond After Heart Attack

After a heart attack, people continue to be at risk for another cardiac event, including another heart attack. Psychosocial factors may contribute to that risk, regardless of the severity of the heart attack. In general, female heart patients suffer more anxiety than men do. Worries over family responsibilities may very well contribute. They may fear the loss of their traditional caregiving roles, upon which much of their self-esteem is based, and this can add to their stress burdens.

Response to Bypass Surgery

To assess the effects of depression on the outcome after coronary artery bypass surgery, researchers followed 207 men and 102 women for a year after surgery. Of these patients, 20 percent were diagnosed with major depressive disorder before being discharged from the hospital. One year later, 27 percent of the depressed patients had suffered a cardiac event, while only 10 percent of the nondepressed patients had suffered a cardiac event. Those with major depression had a 2.3 times greater risk of further cardiac events, while women (without regard to signs of depression) had a 2.4 percent increased risk. The interaction of these two risk factors (having major depression and being female) may be responsible for the less favorable outcome of heart surgery among women.

When comparisons were made between women and men admitted for bypass surgery to five medical centers in the United States and

Canada, the data highlighted the less favorable medical and psychosocial status of women compared to men, repeating much of what is already known in the general population:

- Women having bypass surgery are usually older than men having it.
- Women are more likely than men to have a serious preoperative medical condition.
- After surgery, fewer women than men can perform basic self-care.
- After surgery, fewer women than men can perform the activities required for independent living, running a home, and recreation.
- Women tend to be more anxious than men.
- Women have more depressive symptoms than men.

The Need for Cardiac Rehabilitation

The previous sections point to the importance of cardiac rehabilitation, a therapy provided after coronary bypass surgery that can potentially correct some of these differences. The staffs at cardiac rehabilitation centers need to pay special attention to the home situations of women in their care. Much of women's rehabilitation success depends on the psychological skills and training of the staff. However, women are less likely to enroll in cardiac rehabilitation, and once enrolled, they are more likely than men to drop out and to attend less often. Several reasons exist.

- Physicians tend to recommend cardiac rehabilitation more strongly to men than to women.
- Women are less likely than men to have a car to help them attend the program.
- Women are more likely than men to have dependent family members at home that make it difficult for them to be away for any length of time.

- The worst attendees are likely to be younger women who are single mothers or who have little or no insurance and/or low-paying jobs.
- Older women with no car and a dependent husband also have low attendance records.

The good news is that women who complete a cardiac rehabilitation program show the same or even greater improvement in functional ability than men.

The next chapter is imperative for readers who are considering or who are already taking hormone replacement therapy.

18

Hormone Replacement Therapy for the Heart and Mind

Barbara and her husband of nearly thirty years lived in Ashland, a suburb of Richmond, Virginia. She taught at an elementary school, and he was an administrator with a local university. Their daughter was a freshman in college, and their two sons were in the last two years of high school. At nearly fifty-one, Barbara had begun to have hot flashes, difficulty in sleeping, mood swings, and depression. She found her hot flashes mild and tolerable. But her mood swings, inability to sleep, and depression came in cycles and interfered significantly with her life.

About twenty pounds over her ideal weight, Barbara had a cholesterol level of 235 (200 mg/dL or less is regarded as normal). Although she had always enjoyed excellent health and never smoked, her family had a strong history of heart disease. Her father had died of a massive heart attack at age sixty-seven. Both her mother and older brother had undergone bypass surgery—her mother at seventy-one and her brother at fifty-six. Barbara intended to ask her family doctor whether she should have hormone replacement therapy.

Barbara had heard of the risks of hormone replacement therapy (HRT), as well as its benefits. She felt that she should be responsible for her own health and make her own decision whether to go on therapy, unlike some women she knew who left the decision to their doc-

tors. *In seeking her doctor's advice, Barbara intended to say that the final decision needed to be her own.*

Barbara told her doctor about her hot flashes, difficulty in sleeping, mood swings, and depression. Although she was overweight, had a high cholesterol level, and had a strong family history of heart disease, she had no symptoms of heart disease herself. But her doctor pointed out that Barbara had significant risk factors for coronary artery disease and that hormone replacement therapy could add to them. Therefore, instead of prescribing HRT, he said she needed to lose weight, lower her cholesterol level, and have regular cardiac checkups. For her mood swings and depression, her doctor thought that she should try other strategies before HRT. Barbara had a choice of antidepressants, cognitive behavior therapy, and interpersonal therapy.

HORMONE REPLACEMENT THERAPY after menopause has been prescribed to prevent coronary artery disease, mood swings, depression, cognitive decline, and osteoporosis. However, the medical field now knows that HRT can promote the very things it was meant to prevent. Even when hormone replacement therapy is successful, its risks usually outweigh its benefits. Very recently, however, doctors have been developing modified therapies in which the benefits may prove to outweigh the risks.

Studies in Hormone Replacement Therapy

HRT has been used short term (less than five years) for menopause symptoms and longer term for prevention of heart disease and osteoporosis. Generally, the longer the therapy, the greater the risk of unpleasant side effects. Usually, two hormones are replaced in hormone replacement therapy:

- Estrogen, dominant in the first half of the menstrual cycle (Equine estrogen is used in hormone replacement therapy. Although chemically similar to human estrogen, the two are not identical.)
- Progesterone, dominant in the second half

An Early Look at HRT

When hormone replacement therapy first became widely used by American women in the 1960s and early 1970s, only estrogen was replaced. Research suggested that use of estrogen alone could cause cancer of the endometrium (uterus lining). During a woman's reproductive years, in each menstrual cycle her natural estrogen builds up the uterus lining to receive and nurture a fertilized egg, while progesterone stops this process. Adding artificial progesterone called *progestin* to hormone replacement therapy protects women against unchecked precancerous growth of the endometrium (a condition called *hyperplasia*) and against endometrial cancer. Nowadays, therapy with estrogen alone is recommended primarily for women whose uterus has been removed in a hysterectomy.

Initial Studies on HRT

By 2002, almost four out of ten postmenopausal American women used hormone replacement therapy to protect them from the burden of chronic disease as they grew older. Cardiovascular disease, cancer, osteoporosis, and cognitive decline (often starting with memory loss) were the factors that researchers were trying to prevent or at least delay. With so many women using this therapy, it would have been reasonable to expect that much must be known about its safety and effectiveness. However, this was not so.

Many studies had shown that hormone replacement therapy dramatically reduced the risk of coronary artery disease in postmenopausal women. In a substantial number of these studies, therapy was with estrogen alone. Some therapy was of women *without* coronary disease, called *primary prevention*. Other therapy was of women *with* coronary artery disease, known as *secondary prevention*. While there were some negative studies, favorable studies predominated. This led some doctors to describe the reduction in coronary artery disease with hormone replacement therapy as unprecedented, leading to much optimism. Furthermore, other studies showed that hormone replacement therapy reduced lipids in the blood and blood vessel linings. For a while, it appeared that women's protection against heart disease could be extended beyond menopause. As a result of these reports, more women started on hormone replacement therapy.

Various studies reporting conflicting outcomes were very confusing. Which studies were believable? We can greatly simplify things if we ask what kind of study we are looking at. There are generally two kinds: observational study and prospective, randomized, placebo-controlled study.

Many of the pro-HRT studies were observational. An observational study looks at a group of women that are on hormone replacement therapy and a group of women that are not. The researchers try to make both groups similar, but it is hard to ensure this. For example, do participants on HRT take better care of their health than participants not on HRT? Have they better access to medical care? Does this influence the study's results? Many researchers think so. They believe that the group on therapy is overrepresented by healthy women who take much better care of their health than the average woman.

In a prospective, randomized, placebo-controlled study, researchers have greater ability to ensure that the two groups of women are similar and that women are assigned to either HRT or placebo at random. The results of this kind of study are much less likely to be affected by bias.

The Heart and Estrogen/Progestin Replacement Study (HERS) was the first randomized trial to examine the effects of hormone replacement therapy on women who were already known to have heart disease. The 2,763 women, who averaged sixty-six years old, were randomly assigned to either HRT or a placebo. Their cardiac health was followed up for more than four years. HERS found that hormone replacement therapy provided no protection against coronary artery disease. Death from heart disease and heart attack were similar in both groups. Furthermore, women on hormone replacement therapy had a 50 percent higher risk of coronary artery disease events during the first year of the study.

The Estrogen Replacement and Atherosclerosis (ERA) trial involved therapy with estrogen alone or estrogen in combination with progestin. The researchers did not find that hormone replacement therapy provided any protection in postmenopausal women with known heart disease. Researchers had similar preliminary results for transdermal estradiol in another study.

What about postmenopausal women who did not have coronary artery disease? There was no definitive answer yet. However, most studies had not shown a clear benefit.

The Women's Health Initiative Study: Shocking the Medical World

In July 2002, the federally sponsored Women's Health Initiative study of the popular estrogen-progestin pill Prempro was canceled. This was because findings were so unexpected that researchers did not want to continue to put the study subjects at risk. Preliminary results from the Women's Health Initiative study showed a small increase in heart attacks, stroke, and blood clots during the first year or two among women given hormone replacement therapy with an estrogen-progestin combination. Previous to its surprise cancellation, the results of this ongoing, large-scale, randomized trial were expected in 2005.

In 2002, the sixteen thousand women participating in the Women's Health Initiative study of Prempro received a letter telling them that the study had been abandoned. The cancellation was due to an unacceptably high risk of breast cancer. At that time, about six million American women were taking Prempro, a pill combining estrogen and progestin. Many of the study participants had been taking it for more than five years. During the year ending in May 2002, the drug company Wyeth sold $949 million worth of Prempro and $1.58 billion of Premarin (estrogen only). The study's early results suggested the following for every ten thousand women on estrogen-progestin HRT, in comparison to women not on HRT:

- Eight more will develop invasive breast cancer.
- Seven more will have a heart attack.
- Eight more will have a stroke.
- Eighteen more will have blood clots in the lungs.

While seven, or even eighteen, out of ten thousand women represent only a very small increase, it was unacceptably high for the doctors conducting this medical research. Understandably, the doctors could not condone knowingly endangering the health of the volunteer participants in their study.

There was also good news. The study found the following for every ten thousand women on estrogen-progestin HRT, in comparison to women not on HRT:

- Six fewer will have colorectal cancer.
- Five fewer will have hip fractures.

But were these benefits, along with the feeling of well-being that estrogen-progestin HRT conveys, worth the risks involved? That question was now answered for some women but left unanswered for others. Now, however, they had more reliable data on which to base a decision than ever before. But questions, challenges, and some modifications seemed likely to follow.

A second Women's Health Initiative study was being conducted on HRT with estrogen alone. This study, involving eleven thousand women with hysterectomies, continued. Although the risks and benefits remained uncertain, there was no sign of any increased risk of breast cancer. In the estrogen-progestin study, the threat of breast cancer seemed to arouse a more intense response than the cardiovascular risks, although the cardiovascular risks were higher.

What Doctors Said

Dr. Deborah Grady, director of the University of California at San Francisco/Mount Zion Women's Health Clinical Research Center, said she considered the estrogen-progestin combination a dangerous drug and intended to urge women to stop taking it. She said that if a woman stops taking the drug and her menopausal symptoms return at an unbearable level, she could return to taking the drug for another year and then stop again. But if a woman has been taking the hormone combination for four or more years—the time at which breast cancer becomes a risk—she should gradually reduce her hormone therapy until she can manage without it.

Emory University cardiologist Dr. Nannette Wenger said she could understand the use of the hormone combination to alleviate menopause symptoms but would not recommend it to her patients.

Dr. Lori Mosca, director of preventive cardiology at New York Presbyterian Hospital in New York, said, "If a woman has only been taking hormones for a year or two to treat hot flashes, it's probably safe for her to go on. But if she's been on hormones for ten years, it's time to stop."

Dr. Roger A. Lobo, professor of obstetrics and gynecology at the same medical center, said he often prescribed doses only half as strong as those used in the Women's Health Initiative study. "If a woman wants to take estrogen and progestin for the quality of life," he said, "my recommendation would be that she take the hormones in low doses and that we monitor those doses once or twice a year." He added, "And she should have mammograms once a year."

But for Dr. Maura Parker Quinlan, a specialist in HRT at the University of Chicago Hospitals, the risks of breast cancer and cardiovascular disease outweigh the benefit for bones. Besides, she noted, other safe drugs are available for osteoporosis.

Physician and bestselling author Christiane Northrup said that she intended to continue prescribing low doses of what she called "bioidentical" hormones. She explained that such hormones are exact copies of those secreted in the human body. The estrogen in Prempro is extracted from pregnant mares' urine and is similar but not identical to human estrogen. Bioidentical hormones include the pill Estrace and patches Climara, Estroderm, and Vivelle. They all replace estradiol, a form of estrogen. To replace human progesterone, Prempro uses the similar compound progestin. The pill Prometrium and topical creams Emerita, PhytoGest, and Pro-Gest all use a bioidentical compound to human progesterone. Dr. Northrup warned, however, that none of these products have received the same scrutiny as Prempro.

Today's Modified Therapies

At the beginning of 2004, it was estimated that at least two-thirds of the fifteen million women who were on HRT in 1999 had stopped. Some women, because of the recurrence of severe menopause symptoms when they stopped HRT, returned to it, deciding that the relief of discomfort outweighed the risks.

The risks are real. New evidence has continued to accumulate. In March 2004, the National Institutes of Health announced the halt a year early of its second Women's Health Initiative study, in which participants used estrogen only. The study was abandoned early because the estrogen increased the risk of stroke and offered no protection against heart disease.

For women who need HRT in spite of the risks, doctors are looking into skin patches, flexible vaginal rings, gels, and creams in which the estrogen is not processed by the liver's first-pass metabolism. This may or may not reduce the risk. Among the brand names are Vivelle-Dot and Climara for skin patches, Femring and Estring for vaginal rings, and Estrogel for gels. We are not endorsing these brands. They may turn out to be just as risky as oral HRT. But if you feel that you must have HRT, you might talk to a physician who has had experience with these modified therapies.

When menopause symptoms such as hot flashes and insomnia are severe and interfere with daily activities, hormone replacement therapy may be justifiable, especially if alternatives such as antidepressants, gabapentin (Neurontin), or soy and black cohash have been unsuccessful. Menopause symptoms are short term, however, and the therapy should be also. For symptoms such as depression and mood swings, other remedies should be considered.

There's no justification, however, to go on hormone replacement therapy to prevent coronary artery disease. HRT does not prevent it. The best ways of reducing the risks of heart disease are stopping smoking, losing weight, exercising, eating a healthy diet, taking a cholesterol-lowering medication, and addressing negative emotions.

Epilogue

WE BEGAN THIS BOOK with heartbreak, so it is fitting that the book addresses this sentiment here at the end. Heartbreak is indeed a poignant metaphor, but it is clearly more than just a metaphor. As a heart surgeon and a psychiatrist, we have known or taken care of patients who have succumbed to sudden death, suffered a heart attack, or felt chest pain from profound sadness, anger, anxiety, and stress.

In the United States and many other industrialized nations, coronary artery disease has evolved into the leading cause of illness and death. Likewise, depression and other mental health conditions are exceedingly common. Indeed, depression is the second-most disabling condition, after heart disease, in developed countries. By 2020, it is estimated that this will be true in the developing world as well. The impact of these two conditions on spouses, life partners, families, friends, coworkers, and society in general is enormous and beyond enumeration.

Today, we are all familiar with the risk factors of coronary artery disease: advanced age, high-fat diet, elevated blood levels of cholesterol, high blood pressure, smoking, diabetes, family history, and so on. This book proposes recognizing one more risk factor for serious consideration: depression and other negative emotions.

From this book, you now know in detail how numerous negative emotions, with depression foremost among them, are associated with coronary artery disease and many of its manifestations. You also know about depression's impact following a heart attack or coronary bypass surgery. These adverse outcomes are not just minor complications but may also involve a longer hospital stay, another heart attack, more heart rhythm disturbances, decreased success of the bypass graft, reduced quality of life, and possibly death. While depression has been investigated as the main conspirator, anger, anxiety, social isolation, and stress have been indicted as coconspirators.

Coronary artery disease has received a lot of attention as a major illness. Coronary bypass surgery has become so pervasive that the operation is often taken almost for granted. This is not the case, however, with mental health conditions likely to be associated with heart disease. They remain shrouded in significant misunderstandings, myths, and social stigma. Encouraging greater access to mental health services is an area to which health professionals—especially those primary care physicians on the front lines—and the public can make major contributions in the future. While it has been helpful for some celebrities to bravely come forward to discuss their mental health problems, real progress against the stigma of mental illnesses will be made only when families openly face the issue together in a caring way and then demand parity of insurance coverage so that appropriate professional care can be obtained.

In preventing coronary artery disease through lessening your risk factors, you need to pay attention to depression and certain other negative emotions. There is a simple mind-body medicine equation that is good to keep in mind as you attempt to strengthen your resiliency against both heart disease and depression: propensity to illness is equal to stress as your numerator over social support as your denominator. Many of the studies reviewed in this book show that experiencing increased stress, especially in the setting of social isolation, is a surefire way to increase your odds of developing or exacerbating illnesses like heart disease and depression, particularly if you are among those who have a family history suggesting a genetic vulnerability. Call this your "Heart-Mind Equation" and find ways to reduce your stress and improve your social support.

In a recent article on resiliency from National Institute of Mental Health researcher Dennis Charney, we learn that resilient, healthy individuals are optimistic and find ways to enjoy life. They also find ways to be effective while not letting their anxieties generalize and overcome them. And, in addition, they form secure attachments with family and friends, and, using that reserve of security, they have the goodwill to be altruistic toward others. Some of us have these attributes by virtue of our births and backgrounds, but with the help of relaxation and cognitive behavioral skills training, social support, exercise, and the cultivation of a positive, optimistic, and some would say spiritual outlook on life, all of us can improve our heart-mind equation.

But what if our resiliency falters? As we have seen, the very effective therapies for various forms of heart disease (unstable angina and heart attacks) can be diminished by depression and other negative emotions. Fortunately, there are also effective therapies for depression and other mental health conditions. You must not allow misunderstandings, myths, and social stigma to stand in the way of prompt evaluation and treatment. It is our hope that this book has shown you that for optimal cardiovascular health, you need to acknowledge your emotions and seek to nurture a positive frame of mind.

Resources

General Mental Health

Online information on general and specific mental health conditions:

American Psychiatric Association
www.psych.org

American Psychological Association
www.apa.org

National Alliance for the Mentally Ill (NAMI)
NAMI helpline: 800-950-6264
www.nami.org

National Mental Health Association
800-969-6642
www.nmha.org

Depression

Online information on depression and related topics:

Depression and Related Affective Disorders Association
www.drada.org

National Depressive and Manic Depressive Association
   (support groups in your area)
www.ndmda.org

National Foundation for Depressive Illness
www.depression.org

Anxiety

Online information on anxiety disorders, including panic disorder:

Anxiety Disorders Association of America
www.adaa.org

The Anxiety Network International
www.anxietynetwork.com

The Anxiety Panic Disorder Internet Resource
www.algy.com/anxiety/index.shtml

National Anxiety Foundation
www.lexington-on-line.com/naf.html

Panic Disorders

Online information on panic disorder:

www.geocities.com/hotsprings/spa/8382
www.panicdisorder.about.com

Seasonal Affective Disorders

Online information on SAD:

www.light-and-ion-therapy.org
www.sada.org.uk
www.mentalhealth.com/book/p40-sad.html

Women's Health

Online information on women's health issues:

American Heart Association
www.women.americanheart.org

American Medical Women's Association
www.amwa-doc.org

Microsoft Network
www.womencentral.msn.com

National Women's Health Resource Center
www.healthywomen.org

Newspapers and News

News sites with health information:

BBC's health website
www.bbc.co.uk/health

CBS Healthwatch
www.cbsnews.com

New York Times
Includes excellent articles, but past articles require small purchase
  fee.
www.nytimes.com

General Health

Healthology
www.healthology.com

HeartPoint
www.heartpoint.com

New York Online Access to Health (NOAH)
www.noah-health.org

RxList
www.rxlist.com

WebMD
www.webmd.com

Yahoo's health website
http://health.yahoo.com

Medical Centers and Hospitals

Mayo Clinic
www.mayoclinic.com

University of Cincinnati/Ohio State University/Case Western Reserve
  University
www.netwellness.org

Selected References

Chapter 1: Understanding the Heart-Mind Conspirators

Brinadspiegel, H. Z., et al. 1998. A broken heart. *Circulation* 98:1349.

Penninx, B. W. J. H., et al. 1999. Minor and major depression and the risk of death in older persons. *Arch. Gen. Psychiatry* 56:889–895.

Rozanski, A., et al. 1999. Impact of psychological factors on the pathogenesis of cardiovascular disease and implications for therapy. *Circulation* 99:2192–2217.

Sher, L. 2001. Effects of seasonal mood changes on seasonal variations in coronary heart disease: Role of immune system, infection, and inflammation. *Med. Hypotheses* 56:104–106.

Timberlake, N., et al. 1997. Incidence and patterns of depression following coronary artery bypass graft surgery. *J. Psychosomatic Res.* 43(2):197–207.

Chapter 2: Heart Disease: When the Heart's in Trouble

Challem, J. *The Inflammation Syndrome.* New York: Wiley, 2003.

Hackam, D. G., and S. S. Anand. 2003. Emerging risk factors for atherosclerotic vascular disease. *JAMA* 290:932–940.

Libby, P., et al. 2002. Inflammation and atherosclerosis. *Circulation* 105:1135–1143.

Pearson, T. A., et al. 2003. Markers of inflammation and cardiovascular disease. *Circulation* 197:499–511.

Ross, R. 1999. Atherosclerosis—An inflammatory disease. *N. Engl. J. Med.* 340(2):115–126.

Schneiderman, N., et al. 2001. Health psychology: Psychosocial and biobehavioral aspects of chronic disease management. *Annu. Rev. Psychol.* 52:555–580.

Chapter 3: The Poison Fog of Depression

American Medical Association. *Essential Guide to Depression*. New York: Pocket Books, 1998.

Gallo, J. J., and J. C. Coyne. 2000. The challenge of depression in late life. *JAMA* 284:1570–1572.

The Harvard Medical School Family Health Guide. New York: Simon and Schuster, 2000.

Kramlinger, K. G. *Mayo Clinic on Depression*. New York: Kensington, 2001.

The President's Commission on Mental Health. 1977. Assessing the needs of the nation. *Hospital Community Psychiatry* 28:677–682.

Styron, W. *Darkness Visible*. New York: Random House, 1990.

U.S. Public Health Service. *Call to Action to Prevent Suicide*. Washington, D.C.: U.S. Government Printing Office, 1999.

Chapter 4: Depression's Link to Coronary Artery Disease

Anda, R., et al. 1993. Depressed affect, hopelessness, and the risk of ischemic heart disease in a cohort of U.U. adults. *Epidemiology* 4:285–294.

Ariyo, A. A., et al. 2000. Depressive symptoms and risks of coronary heart disease and mortality in elderly Americans. *Circulation* 102:1773–1779.

Barefoot, J. C., et al. 1996. Depression and long-term mortality risk in patients with coronary artery disease. *Am. J. Cardiol.* 78:613–617.

Bush, D. E., et al. 2001. Even minimal symptoms of depression increase cardiac mortality risk after acute myocardial infarction. *Am. J. Cardiol.* 88:337–341.

Doulalas, A. D., et al. Association of depressive symptoms with coagulation factors in young healthy individuals. *Atherosclerosis* Jul 30 (2005), www.sciencedirect.com.

Engel-Arieli, S. L. *How Your Body Works.* Emeryville, CA: Ziff-Davis Press, 1994.

Ferketich, A. K., et al. 2000. Depression as an antecedent to heart disease among women and men in the NHANES I study. *Arch. Intern. Med.* 160:1261–1268.

Ford, D. E., et al. 1998. Depression is a risk factor for coronary artery disease in men: The Precursors Study. *Arch. Intern. Med.* 158:1422–1426.

Glassman, A. H., and T. A. Shapiro. 1998. Depression in the course of coronary artery disease. *Am. J. Psychiatry* 155:4–11.

Hippisley-Cox, J., et al. 1998. Depression as a risk factor for ischemic heart disease in men: Population based case-control study. *Brit. Med. J.* 316:1714–1719.

Lesperance, F., et al. 2000. Depression and 1-year prognosis in unstable angina. *Arch. Intern. Med.* 160:1354–1360.

Maes, M., R. Smith, and S. Scharpe. 1995. The monocyte T-lymphocyte hypothesis of major depression. *Psychoneuroendocrinology* 20:111–116.

Musselman, D. L., et al. 1998. The relationship of depression to cardiovascular disease. *Arch. Gen. Psychiatry* 55:580–592.

Notelovitsz, M., and D. Tonnessen. *The Essential Heart Book for Women.* New York: St. Martin's Press, 1996.

O'Malley, P. G., et al. 2000. Lack of correlation between psychological factors and subclinical coronary artery disease. *N. Engl. J. Med.* 343:1298–1304.

Penninx, B. W. J. H., et al. 1999. Minor and major depression and the risk of death in older persons. *Arch. Gen. Psychiatry* 56:889–895.

Pickering, T., et al. 2001. Letter. *N. Engl. J. Med.* 344:608–609.

Pratt, L., et al. 1996. Depression, psychotropic medication, and risk of myocardial infarction: Prospective data from the Baltimore ECA follow-up. *Circulation* 94:3123–3129.

Rosen, S. D., et al. 1996. Silent ischemia as a central problem: Regional brain activation compared in silent and painful myocardial ischemia. *Ann. Intern. Med.* 124:939–949.

Soteriades, E. S. 2001. Letter. *N. Engl. J. Med.* 344:609.

Chapter 5: When Depression Comes After a Heart Attack

Appels, A., and P. Mulder. 1988. Excess fatigue as a precursor of myocardial infarction. *Eur. Heart J.* 9:758–764.

Bush, D. E., et al. 2001. Even minimal symptoms of depression increase cardiac mortality risk after acute myocardial infarction. *Am. J. Cardiol.* 88:337–341.

Crowe, J. M., et al. 1996. Anxiety and depression after acute myocardial infarction. *Heart Lung* 25:98–107.

Frasure-Smith, N., et al. 1993. Depression following myocardial infarction: Impact on 6-month survival. *JAMA* 270:1819–1825.

Frasure-Smith, N., et al. 1995. Depression and 18-month prognosis after myocardial infarction. *Circulation* 91:999–1005.

Frasure-Smith, N., et al. 1995. The impact of negative emotions on prognosis following myocardial infarction: Is it more than depression? *Health Psychol.* 14(5):388–398.

The Harvard Medical School Family Health Guide. New York: Simon & Schuster, 2000.

Januzzi, J. L., et al. 2000. The influence of anxiety and depression on outcome of patients with coronary artery disease. *Arch. Intern. Med.* 160:1913–1921.

Lane, D., et al. 2001. Mortality and quality of life 12 months after myocardial infarction: Affects of depression and anxiety. *Psychosomatic Med.* 63:221–230.

Lesperance, F., et al. 1996. Major depression before and after myocardial infarction: Its nature and consequences. *Psychosomatic Med.* 58:99–110.

Nagourney, E. In heart disease, head can be an ally. *New York Times*, Nov. 27, 2001.

Chapter 6: Depression Before and After Bypass Surgery

Baker, R. A., et al. 2001. Preoperative depression and mortality in coronary artery bypass surgery: Preliminary findings. *A. N. Z. J. Surg.* 71(3):139–142.

Connerney, I., et al. 2001. Relation between depression after coronary artery bypass surgery and 12-month outcome: A prospective study. *Lancet* 358:1766–1771.

DeBakey, M. E., and A. M. Gotto. *The New Living Heart.* Holbrook, MA: Adams, 1997.

Eriksson, M., et al. 2002. Delirium after coronary bypass surgery evaluated by the organic brain syndrome protocol. *Scand Cardiovasc J.* 36(4):250–5.

Jacobs, A., et al. 1998. Alterations of neuropsychological function and cerebral glucose metabolism after cardiac surgery are not related only to intraoperative microembolic elements. *Stroke* 29:660–667.

Khatri, P., et al. 1999. Perception of cognitive function in older adults following coronary artery bypass surgery. *Health Psychol.* 18(3):301–306.

McKhann, G. M., et al. 1997. Depression and cognitive decline after coronary artery bypass grafting. *Lancet* 349:1282–1284.

Moller, J. T. 1998. Long-term postoperative cognitive dysfunction in the elderly: ISPOCDI study. *Lancet* 351:857–861.

Newman, S. P., et al. 1989. Subjective reports of cognition in relation to assessed cognitive performance following CABG. *J. Psychosomatic Res.* 33:227–233.

Oxman, T., et al. 1995. Lack of social participation or religious strength and comfort as risk factors for death after cardiovascular surgery in the elderly. *Psychosomatic Med.* 57:5–15.

Perski, A., et al. 1998. Emotional distress before coronary artery bypass grafting limits the benefits of surgery. *Am. Heart J.* 136(3):510–517.

Pirraglia, P. P., et al. 1999. Depressive symptomatology in coronary artery bypass graft surgery patients. *Int. J. Geriat. Psychiatry* 14:668–680.

Roach, G. W., et al. 1996. Adverse cerebral outcomes after coronary artery bypass surgery. *N. Engl. J. Med.* 335:1857–1863.

Sauer, C. D., et al. 2001. Depressive symptoms and outcome of coronary artery bypass grafting. *Am. J. Crit. Care* 10(1):4–10.

Scheier, M. F., et al. 1999. Optimism and rehospitalization after coronary artery bypass graft surgery. *Arch. Intern. Med.* 159(8):829–835.

Selnes, O. A., et al. 1999. Neurobehavioral sequelae of cardiopulmonary bypass. *Lancet.* 353(9164):1601–1606.

Selnes, O. A., et al. 2001. Coronary artery bypass surgery and the brain. *N. Engl. J. Med.* 344:451–452.

Timberlake, N., et al. 1996. Incidence and patterns of depression following coronary artery bypass graft surgery. *J. Psychosomatic Res.* 43(2):197–207.

Van der Mast, R. C., et al. 2000. Is delirium after cardiac surgery related to plasma amino acids and physical condition? *J. Neuropsychiatry Clin. Neurosci.* 12:57–63.

Chapter 7: Anxiety: Going to the Heart of the Matter

Frasure-Smith, N., et al. 1995. The impact of negative emotions on prognosis following myocardial infarction: Is it more than depression? *Health Psychol.* 14:388–398.

Haines, A. P., et al. 1987. Phobic anxiety and ischemic heart disease. *BMJ Clin. Res. Ed.* 295:297–299.

Januzzi, J. L., et al. 2000. The influence of anxiety and depression on outcomes of patients with coronary artery disease. *Arch. Intern. Med.* 160:1913–1921.

Kawachi, I., et al. 1994. Prospective study of phobic anxiety and risk of coronary heart disease in men. *Circulation* 89:1992–1997.

Kawachi, I., et al. 1994. Symptoms of anxiety and risk of coronary heart disease: The Normative Aging Study. *Circulation* 90:2225–2229.

Kubzansky, L. D., et al. 1997. Is worrying bad for your heart? A prospective study of worry and coronary heart disease in the Normative Aging Study. *Circulation* 95:818–824.

Kubzansky, L. D., and I. Kawachi. 2000.Going to the heart of the matter: Do negative emotions cause coronary heart disease? *J. Psychosom. Med.* 48:323–337.

Moser, D. K., and K. Dracup. 1996. Is anxiety early after myocardial infarction associated with subsequent ischemic and arrhythmic events? *Psychosom. Med.* 58:395–401.

Rozanski, A., et al. 1999. Impact of psychological factors on the pathogenesis of cardiovascular disease and implications for therapy. *Circulation* 99:2192–2217.

Shemesh, E., et al. 2001. *Gen. Hospital Psychiatry* 23:215–222.

Weissman, M. M., et al. 1990. Panic disorders and cardiovascular/cerebrovascular problems: Results from a community survey. *Am. J. Psychiatry* 147:1504–1508.

Chapter 8: Anger: The Most Damaging Component of a Type A Personality

Angerer, P., et al. 2000. Impact of social support, cynical hostility and anger expression on progression of coronary atherosclerosis. *J. Am. Coll. Cardiol.* 36:1781–1788.

Anson, G., et al. 1992. Anger and left ventricular ejection fraction in coronary artery disease. *Am. J. Cardiol.* 70:281–285.

Boltwood, M. D., et al. 1993. Anger report predicts coronary artery vasomotor response to mental stress in atherosclerotic segments. *Am. J. Cardiol.* 72:1362–1365.

Denollet, J., and D. L. Brutsaert. 1998. Personality, disease severity, and the risk of long-term cardiac events in patients with a decreased ejection fraction after myocardial infarction. *Circulation* 97:167–173.

Hemmingway, H., and M. Marmot. 1999. Psychosocial factors in the aetiology and prognosis of coronary heart disease: Systematic review of prospective cohort studies. *BMJ* 318:1460–1467.

Kaplan, J. R., et al. 1983. Social stress and atherosclerosis in normocholesterolemic monkey. *Science* 220:733–735.

Kaufmann, M. W., et al. 1999. Relation between myocardial infarction, depression, hostility and death. *Am. Heart J.* 138:549–554.

Kawachi, I., et al. 1996. A prospective study of anger and coronary artery disease: The Normative Aging Study. *Circulation* 94:2090–2095.

Mittleman, M. A., et al. 1995. Triggering of acute myocardial infarction onset by episodes of anger. *Circulation* 92:1720–1725.

Watson, B., and L. A. Clark. 1984. Negative affectivity: A disposition to experience adverse emotional states. *Psychol. Bull.* 96:465–490.

Wielgosz, A. T., and R. P. Nolan. 2000. Behavioral factors in the context of ischemic cardiovascular diseases. *J. Psychosom. Res.* 48:339–345.

Chapter 9: Social Isolation: No Man (or Woman) Is an Island

Berkman, L. F. 1995. The role of social relations in health promotion. *Psychosom. Med.* 57:245–254.

Berkman, L. F., et al. 1992. Emotional support and survival after myocardial infarction: A prospective, population-based study of the elderly. *Ann. Int. Med.* 117:1003–1009.

Case, R. B., et al. 1992. Living alone after myocardial infarction. *JAMA* 267:515–519.

Cohen, S., and L. Syme, eds. *Social Support in Health.* Orlando, FL: Academic Press, 1985.

Crumholz, H. M., et al. 1998. The prognostic importance of emotional support for elderly patients hospitalized with heart failure. *Circulation* 97:958–964.

Forde, E. S., et al. 2000. Social relationships and cardiovascular disease risk factors: Findings from the National Health and Nutrition Examination Survey III. *Prevent. Med.* 30:83–92.

Frasure-Smith, N., and F. Lesperance. 2000. Coronary artery disease, depression and social support: Only the beginning. *Eur. Heart J.* 21:1043–1045.

Frasure-Smith, N., et al. 2000. Social support, depression and mortality during the first year following myocardial infarction. *Circulation* 101:1919–1924.

Glaser, R., et al. 1992. Stress induced modulation of the immune response to recombinant hepatitis B vaccine. *Psychosom. Med.* 54:22–29.

Helminen, A., et al. 1995. Carotid atherosclerosis in middle-aged men: Relation to conjugal circumstances and social support. *Scand. J. Soc. Med.* 23:167–172.

Hirsch, B. J., and D. I. Dubois. 1992. Social support in psychological symptomatology during the transition to junior high school: A two-year longitudinal analysis. *Am. J. Community Psychol.* 20:333–347.

Horsten, M., et al. 2000. Depressive symptoms and lack of social integration in relation to prognosis of CHD in middle-aged women: The Stockholm Female Coronary Risk Study. *Eur. Heart J.* 21:1072–1080.

Idler, E., and F. Kasl. 1997. Religion among disabled and non-disabled persons, II: Attendance at religious services as a predictor of a course of disability. *J. Gerontol. Ser. D Psychol. Sci. Soc. Sci.* 52:S306–S316.

Institute of Medicine. *Health and Behavior: The Interplay of Biological, Behavioral and Societal Influences.* Washington, DC: National Academy Press, 2001.

Kaark, J., et al. 1996. Does religious observance promote health? Mortality in secular vs. religious kibbutzim in Israel. *Am. J. Public Health* 86:341–346.

Lepore, S. J., et al. 1993. Social support lowers cardiovascular reactivity in an acute stressor. *Psychosom. Med.* 55:518–524.

McEwen, B. S. 1996. Impact of social environment characteristics on neuroendocrine regulation. *Psychosom. Med.* 58:459–471.

Orth-Gomer, K., et al. 1998. Socialized relation and mortality in ischemic heart disease. *Acta Scand.* 224:205–215.

Oxman, T. E., et al.1995. Lack of social participation in religious strength and comfort as risk factors for death after cardiac surgery in the elderly. *Psychosom. Med.* 57:5–15.

Rhodes, J. E., et al. 1994. Natural mentor relationships among Latino adolescent mothers: Psychological adjustment moderating processes in the role of early parental acceptance. *Am. J. Community Psychol.* 22:211–227.

Ruberman, W., et al. 1984. Psychosocial influences on mortality after myocardial infarction. *N. Engl. J. Med.* 311:552–559.

Ryff, C. D., and B. Singer, eds. *Emotion, Social Relationships and Health.* New York: Oxford, 2000.

Seeman, T. 1996. Social ties in health: The benefits of social integration. *Ann. Epidemiol.* 6:442–451.

Stefano, G. B., et al. 2001. The placebo effect and relaxation response: Neuro processes and their coupling to nitric oxide. *Brain Res. Rev.* 35:1–19.

Strawbridge, W., et al. 1997. Frequent attendance at religious services and mortality over 28 years. *Am. J. Public Health* 87:957–961.

Taylor, S. E., et al. 1997. Health psychology: What is an unhealthy environment and how does it get under our skin? *Annu. Rev. Psychol.* 48:411–447.

Walker, K. N., et al. 1977. Social support network in the crisis of bereavement. *Soc. Sci. Med.* 11:35–41.

Williams, R., et al. 1992. Prognostic importance of social and economic resources among medically treated patients with angiographically documented coronary artery disease. *JAMA* 267:520–524.

Chapter 10: Two Stress Conspirators

Blumenthal, J. A., et al. 1995. Mental stress-induced ischemia in the laboratory and ambulatory ischemia during daily life. *Circulation* 92:2102–2108.

Chem, D. Principles of stress management. In *The MGH Guide to Psychiatry in Primary Care*, eds. T. Stern, J. B. Herman, and P. L. Slavin. New York: McGraw-Hill, 1998, 39–45.

DeSilva, R. A. 1983. Central nervous system risk factors for sudden cardiac deaths. *J.S.C. Med. Assoc.* 79(10):561–572.

Dwyer, J. H., et al. 2001. Stressful jobs may increase vascular disease risk in men. *Epidemiology* 12:180–185.

Guyton, A. C. *Basic Neuroscience: Anatomy and Physiology.* Philadelphia: Saunders, 1987.

Hlatky, M. A., et al. 1995. Job strain and the prevalence and outcome of coronary artery disease. *Circulation* 92:327–333.

Institute of Medicine. *Health and Behavior: The Interplay of Biological, Behavioral and Societal Influences.* Washington, DC: National Academy Press, 2001.

Kaplan, J. R., et al. 1987. Inhibition of coronary atherosclerosis by propranolol in behaviorally predisposed monkeys fed an atherogenic diet. *Circulation* 76:1365–1372.

Krantz, D. S., et al. 2000. Effects of mental stress in patients with coronary artery disease: Evidence and clinical implications. *JAMA* 283(14):1800.

Leor, J., et al. 1996. Sudden cardiac death triggered by an earthquake. *N. Engl. J. Med.* 334:413–419.

Littman, A. Smoking cessation strategies. In *The MGH Guide to Psychiatry in Primary Care*, eds. T. Stern, J. B. Herman, and P. L. Slavin. New York: McGraw-Hill, 1998, 575–581.

Lown, B. 1979. Sudden cardiac death: The major challenge confronting contemporary cardiology. *Am. J. Cardiol.* 43:313–328.

Lown, B., and R. Verrier. 1976. Neuroactivity in ventricular fibrillation. *N. Engl. J. Med.* 294:1165–1170.

Lown, B., et al. 1997. Neuro and psychological mechanisms for the problem of sudden cardiac deaths. *Am. J. Cardiol.* 39:890–902.

Manuck, S. B., et al. 1988. Effects of stress and the sympathetic nervous system on coronary artery atherosclerosis in the cynomolgus macaque. *Am. Heart J.* 116:328–333.

McEwen, B. 2000. The neurobiology of stress: From serendipity to clinical relevance. *Brain Res.* 886:172–189.

McEwen, B. S. 1998. Protective and damaging effects of stress mediators. *N. Engl. J. Med.* 338:171–179.

Moore, L., et al. 1999. Psychological stress and incidence of ischemic heart disease. *Int. J. Epidemiol.* 28:652–658.

Moss, R., and V. Tsu. The crisis of physical illness: An overview. In *Coping with Physical Illness*, ed. R. Moss. New York: Plenum Press, 1977, 3–21.

Muller, J. E., and R. L. Verrier. 1996. Triggering of sudden death: Lessons from an earthquake. *N. Engl. J. Med.* 334:460–461.

Raikkonen, K., et al. 1996. Association of chronic stress with plasminogen activator inhibitor-1 in healthy middle-aged men. *Arterioscl. Thromb. Vasc. Biol.* 16:363–367.

Rozanski, A., et al. 1988. Mental stress in the induction of silent myocardial ischemia in patients with coronary artery disease. *N. Engl. J. Med.* 318:1005–1012.

Rozanski, A., et al. 1999. Impact of psychological factors on the pathogenesis of cardiovascular disease and implications for therapy. *Circulation* 99:2192–2217.

Schwartz, T., and H. Stone. 1982. The role of the autonomic nervous system in sudden coronary deaths. *Ann. NY Acad. Sci.* 382:162–180.

Zipes, D. P., and H. J. J. Wellens. 1998. Sudden cardiac death. *Circulation* 98:2334–2351.

Chapter 11: Panic Disorder: When Fear Takes Hold

Alpert, M. A., et al. 1991. Mitral valve prolapse, panic disorder, and chest pain. *Med. Clin. North Am.* 75:1119–1133.

Campbell, C., and D. Storz. A 26-year-old woman with heart palpitations. www.medscape.com.

Carney, R. M., et al. 1990. Major depression, panic disorder, and mitral valve prolapse in patients who complain of chest pain. *Am. J. Med.* 89:757–760.

Coplan, J. D. 1992. Amelioration of mitral valve prolapse after treatment for panic disorder. *Am. J. Psychiatry* 149:1587–1578.

Devereux, R. B. 1989. Diagnosis and prognosis of mitral valve prolapse. *N. Engl. J. Med.* 320:1077–1079.

Fleet, R., et al. 2000. Is panic disorder associated with coronary artery disease? A critical review of the literature. *J. Psychosom. Res.* 48:347–356.

Gorman, J. M., et al. 1988. The mitral valve prolapse-panic disorder connection. *Psychosom. Med.* 50:114–122.

Gottlieb, S. H. 1987. Mitral valve prolapse: From syndrome to disease. *Am. J. Cardiol.* 60:53J–58J.

Hamada, T., et al. 1998. Mitral valve prolapse and autonomic function in panic disorder. *Acta Psychiatr. Scand.* 97:139–143.

Heger, J. W., J. T. Niemann, and J. M. Criley. *Cardiology for the House Officer*, 2nd ed. Philadelphia: Williams & Wilkins, 1987, 187–190.

Margraf, J., A. Ehlers, and W. R. Roth. 1988. Mitral valve prolapse and panic disorder: A review of their relationship. *Psychosom. Med.* 50:93–113.

Yang, S., et al. 1997. The effect of panic attack on mitral valve prolapse. *Acta Psychiatr. Scand.* 96:408–411.

Chapter 12: Why So SAD? Daily and Seasonal Rhythms

Kloner, R. A., et al. 1999. When throughout the year is coronary death most likely to occur? A 12-year population-based analysis of more than 220,000 cases. *Circulation* 100:1630–1634.

Partonen, T., and J. Lonnqvist. 1998. Seasonal affective disorder. *Lancet* 352:1369–1374.

Pell, J. P., and S. M. Cobbe. 1999. Seasonal variations in coronary heart disease. *OJM* 92:689–696.

Sher, L. 2001. Effects of seasonal mood changes on seasonal variations in coronary heart disease: Role of immune system, infection, and inflammation. *Med. Hypotheses* 56:104–106.

Wong, C. M., et al. 1999. Coronary artery disease varies seasonably in subtropics. *BMJ* 319:1004.

Zipes, D. P. 1999. Warning: The short days of winter may be hazardous to your health. *Circulation* 100:1590–1592.

Chapter 13: Survival Strategies for Heart Patients

Ades, P. A. 2001. Cardiac rehabilitation and secondary prevention of coronary heart disease. *N. Engl. J. Med.* 345:892–902.

Ai, A. L., et al. 1998. The role of private prayer and psychological recovery among mid-life and aged patients following cardiac surgery. *Gerontologist* 38:591–601.

Annesi, J. J. 2005. Changes in depressed mood associated with 10 weeks of moderate coardiovascular exercise in formerly sedentary adults. *Psychol Rep* 96:855–862.

Berkman L. F., et al. 2003. Effects of treating depression and low perceived social support on clinical events after myocardial infarction: The Enhancing Recovery Coronary Heart Disease Patients (ENRICHD) Randomized Trial. *JAMA* 18:3106–3116.

Bernardi, L., et al. 2001. *BMJ* 323:1446–1449.

Blumenthal, J. A., et al. 1997. Stress management and exercise training in cardiac patients with mild cardiac ischemia. *Arch. Int. Med.* 157:2213–2223.

Casey, A., and H. Benson. *Mind Your Heart: A Mind/Body Approach to Stress Management, Exercise, and Nutrition for Heart Health.* New York: The Free Press, 2004.

Fricchione, G., and E. Marcantonio. Approach to the patient with chronic medical illness. In *The Mass. General Hospital: Psychiatry for the Primary Care Physician Handbook.* New York: McGraw-Hill, 1998, 199–206.

Fricchione, G. L., and S. C. Vlay. Psychiatric aspects of the implantable cardioverter defibrillator. In *Cardioverter Defibrillator: A Comprehensive Text*, eds. N. A. M. Estes, and M. A. Wang. New York: Marcel Dekker, 1994, 405–423.

Hackett, T., and N. Cassem. 1982. Coping with cardiac disease. *Advan. Cardiol.* 31:212–217.

Hedback, D., et al. 1993. Long-term reduction of cardiac mortality after myocardial infarction: Ten-year results of a comprehensive rehabilitation program. *Eur. Heart J.* 14:831–835.

Januzzi, J. L., et al. 2000. The influence of anxiety and depression on outcomes of patients with coronary artery disease. *Arch. Int. Med.* 160:1913–1921.

Linden, W., et al. 1996. Psychosocial intervention for patients with coronary artery disease: A meta analysis. *Arch. Int. Med.* 156:745–752.

Milani, R. V., et al. 1996. Effects of cardiac rehabilitation and exercise training program on depression in patients after major coronary events. *Am. Heart J.* 132:726–732.

Oldridge, M. B., et al. 1988. Cardiac rehabilitation after myocardial infarction: Combined experience of randomized clinical trials. *JAMA* 260:945–950.

Williams, R. B. 1999. A sixty-nine year old man with anger and angina. *JAMA* 282:763–770.

Chapter 14: Treating Depression and Helping the Heart

Brown, G. K., et al. 2005. Cognitive therapy for the prevention of suicide attempts: a randomized controlled trial. *JAMA* 294:623–624.

Fricchione, G. L., et al. Catatonia, neuroleptic malignant syndrome, and serotonin syndrome. In *The Massachusetts General Hospital Handbook of General Hospital Psychiatry*, 5th Ed., eds. T. A. Stern, G. L. Fricchione, N. H. Cassem, M. J. Jellinek, J. F. Rosenbaum. Philadelphia: Mosby-Elsevier, 2004, 513–530.

Miere, C. R., et al. 2001. Use of selective serotonin reuptake inhibitors in risk of developing first time acute myocardial infarction. *Brit. J. Clin. Pharm.* 52:179–184.

Otto, M. W., et al. Cognitive behavioral therapy. In *The McGraw-Hill Guide to Psychiatry and Primary Care*, eds. T. A. Stern, J. P. Harmon, and B. L. Slavin. New York: McGraw-Hill, 1998, 543–547.

Roose, S. P., et al. 1991. Cardiovascular effects of bupropion in depressed patients with heart disease. *Am. J. Psychiatry* 148:512–516.

Roose, S. P., et al. 1998. Cardiovascular effects of fluoxetine in depressed patients with heart disease. *Am. J. Psychiatry* 155:660–665.

Serebruany, B. L., et al. 2001. Platelet inhibition by sertraline in N-demethylsertraline: A possible missing link between depression, coronary events and mortality benefits to selective serotonin reuptake inhibitors. *Pharm. Res.* 43:453–462.

Shapiro, P. A., et al. 1999. An open label preliminary trial of sertraline for treatment of major depression after acute myocardial infarction (the SADHAT trial). *Am. Heart J.* 137:1100–1106.

Whooley, N. A., and G. E. Simon. 2000. Managing depression in medical outpatients. *N. Engl. J. Med.* 343:1942–1950.

Chapter 15: A Healthy Heart Takes a Healthy Mind

Simon, H. B. *Conquering Heart Disease: New Ways to Live Well Without Drugs or Surgery.* Boston: Little, Brown, 1994.

Chapter 16: Women's Hearts

Clarke, K. W., et al. 1994. Do women with acute myocardial infarction receive the same treatment as men? *BMJ* 309:563–566.

Douglas, P. S., and G. S. Ginsburg. 1996. The evaluation of chest pain in women. *N. Engl. J. Med.* 334:1311–1315.

Harvard Women's Health Watch, December 1999, 3–4.

Henig, R. M. Taking care of everybody but herself. *New York Times*, June 24, 2001.

Hogue, C. W., Jr., et al. 2001. Sex differences in neurological outcomes and mortality after cardiac surgery: A Society of Thoracic Surgery National Database Report. *Circulation* 103:2133–2137.

Ladwig, K.-H., et al. 2000. Gender differences in emotional disability and negative health perception in cardiac patients 6 months after stent implantation. *J. Psychosom. Res.* 48:501–508.

Mosca, L., et al. 1997. Cardiovascular disease in women: A statement for healthcare professionals from the American Heart Association. *Circulation* 96:2468–2482.

Mosca, L., et al. 1999. Guide to preventive cardiology for women. *Circulation* 99:2480–2484.

Nabel, E. G. 2000. Coronary heart disease in women: An ounce of prevention, *N. Engl. J. Med.* 343:572–574.

Pilote, L., and M. A. Hlatky. 1995. Attitudes of women toward hormone therapy and prevention of heart disease. *Am. Heart J.* 129:1237–1238.

Rich-Edwards, J. W., et al. 1995. The primary prevention of coronary heart disease in women. *N. Engl. J. Med.* 332:1749–1765.

Sullivan, A. K., et al. 1994. Chest pain in women: Clinical, investigative, and prognostic features. *BMJ* 308:883–886.

Wenger, N. K. 1996. The high risk of CHD for women: Understanding why prevention is crucial. *Medscape Women's Health* 1:6.

Wenger, N. K. 1997. Coronary heart disease: An older woman's major health risk. *BMJ* 315:1085–1090.

Westin, L., et al. 1999. Differences in quality of life in men and women with ischemic heart disease. *Scand. Cardiovasc. J.* 33:160–165.

Chapter 17: The Effects of Stress and Depression on Women's Hearts

Ai, A. L., et al. 1997. How gender affects psychological adjustment one year after coronary artery bypass graft surgery. *J. Women's Health* 26:45–65.

Bogg, J., et al. 2000. Gender variability in mood, quality of life and coping following primary myocardial infarction. *Coronary Health Care* 4:163–168.

Brezinka, V., et al. 1998. Gender differences in psychosocial profile at entry into cardiac rehabilitation. *J. Cardiopulmonary Rehabil.* 18:445–449.

Connerney, I., et al. 2001. Relation between depression after coronary artery bypass surgery and 12-month outcome: A prospective study. *Lancet* 358:1766–1771.

Czajkowski, S. M., et al. 1997. Comparison of preoperative characteristics of men and women undergoing coronary artery bypass grafting: The Post Coronary Artery Bypass Graft (CABG) Biobehavioral Study. *Am. J. Cardiol.* 79:1017–1024.

Engstrom, G., et al. 2000. Incidence of myocardial infarction in women: A cohort study of risk factors and modifiers of effects. *J. Epidemiol. Community Health* 54:104–107.

Ferketich, A. K., et al. 2000. Depression as an antecedent to heart disease among women and men in the NHANES I study. *Arch. Intern. Med.* 160:1261–1268.

Kubzansky, L. D., and I. Kawachi. 2000. Going to the heart of the matter: Do negative emotions cause coronary heart disease? *J. Psychosom. Res.* 48:323–337.

Leibenluft, E. Why are so many women depressed? *Sci. Am.* June 1998.

Maes, M. 1999. Major depression and activation of the inflammatory response system. *Adv. Exp. Med. Biol.* 461:25–46.

Maes, M., et al. 2002. Depressive and anxiety symptoms in the early puerperium are related to increased degradation of tryptophan into kynurenine, a phenomenon which is related to immune activation. *Life Sci.* 71:1837–1848.

Orth-Gomer, K., et al. 1998. Social relations and extent and severity of coronary artery disease: The Stockholm Female Coronary Risk Study. *Eur. Heart J.* 19:1648–1656.

Westin, L., et al. 1999. Differences in quality of life in men and women with ischemic heart disease. *Scand. Cardiovasc. J.* 33:160–165.

Chapter 18: Hormone Replacement Therapy for the Heart and Mind

Barrett-Connor, E. 1998. Hormone replacement therapy. *BMJ* 317:457–461.

Barrett-Connor, E., and D. Grady. 1998. Hormone replacement therapy, heart disease and other considerations. *Annu. Rev. Public Health* 19:55–72.

Belchets, P. E. 1994. Drug therapy: Hormonal treatment of postmenopausal women. *N. Engl. J. Med.* 330:1062–1071.

Burton, T. M. Hormone conundrum. *Wall Street Journal*, July 10, 2002.

Clarke, S., et al. 2000. Transdermal hormone replacement therapy for secondary prevention of coronary artery disease in postmenopausal women. *Eur. Heart J.* 21(Suppl.):212.

Clemons, M., and P. Gross. 2001. Mechanisms of disease: Estrogen and the risk of breast cancer. *N. Engl. J. Med.* 344:276–285.

Collaborative Group on Hormonal Factors in Breast Cancer. 1997. Breast cancer and hormone replacement therapy: Collaborative reanalysis of data from 51 epidemiological studies of 52,705 women with breast cancer and 108,4011 women without breast cancer. *Lancet* 350:1047–1059.

Duenwald, M. Patients weigh quitting drug after research indicates risk. *New York Times*, July 10, 2002.

Eastell, R. 2001. Drug therapy: Treatment of postmenopausal osteoporosis. *N. Engl. J. Med.* 338:736–746.

Grodstein, F., et al. 1997. Postmenopausal hormone therapy and mortality. *N. Engl. J. Med.* 336:1769–1775.

Harvard Women's Health Watch, April 2000, 1–3.

Hensley, S. Wyeth CEO: Concerned but hopeful. *Wall Street Journal*, July 10, 2002.

Herrington, D. M., et al. 2000. Effects of estrogen replacement on the progression of coronary-artery atherosclerosis. *N. Engl. J. Med.* 343:522–529.

Hulley, S., et al. 1998. Randomized trial of estrogen plus progestin for secondary prevention of coronary heart disease in postmenopausal women. *JAMA* 280:605–613.

Jaffe, K., et al. 2001. Cognitive function in postmenopausal women treated with raloxifene. *N. Engl. J. Med.* 344:1207–1213.

Johnson, R. R., and M. E. Sweeney. 2000. Debate: The potential role of estrogen in the prevention of heart disease in women after menopause. *Curr. Control Trials Cardiovasc. Med.* 1:139–142.

Kolata, G. Study is halted over rise seen in cancer risk. *New York Times*, July 9, 2002.

Kolata, G., and M. Petersen. Hormone replacement study a shock to the medical system. *New York Times*, July 10, 2002.

LaRosa, J. H. Current status of hormone replacement therapy for the prevention of heart disease. http://cardiology.medscape.com.

Lenfant, C. *Preliminary Trends in the Women's Health Initiative.* Bethesda, MD: National Heart, Lung, and Blood Institute Communications Office, 2000.

Manson, J. E., and K. A. Martin. 2001. Postmenopausal hormone-replacement therapy. *N. Engl. J. Med.* 345:34–40.

Mayeux, R. 2001. Can estrogen or estrogen-receptor modulators preserve cognitive function in elderly women? *N. Engl. J. Med.* 344:1242–1244.

Mendelsohn, M. E., and R. H. Karas. 1999. Mechanisms of disease: The protective effects of estrogen on the cardiovascular system. *N. Engl. J. Med.* 340:180–181.

Menopause. www.nih.gov/health/chip/nis/menopa/men4.htm.

Postmenopausal Estrogen/Progestin Interventions (PEPI) Trial. 1995. Effects of estrogen or estrogen/progestin regimens on heart disease risk factors in postmenopausal women. *JAMA* 273:199–208.

Schairer, C., et al. 2000. Menopausal estrogen and estrogen-progestin replacement therapy and breast cancer risk. *JAMA* 283:485–491.

Winslow, R., and G. Anand. More options and unknowns. *Wall Street Journal*, July 10, 2002.

Index

Page numbers followed by *t* refer to a table.

221

About the Authors

WINDSOR TING, M.D., is a cardiac surgeon with a busy private practice in New York City. Dr. Ting's special interest in the relationship between emotions and heart disease has led to an innovative approach to the treatment of his patients with heart disease. He is a former assistant professor of surgery at Columbia University and previously taught at Robert Wood Johnson Medical School and the University of Illinois School of Medicine in Chicago. Dr. Ting received his M.D. from Tufts University School of Medicine in Boston, completed his cardiovascular fellowship at College of Physicians and Surgeons at Columbia University, and is board certified in cardiothoracic surgery with additional qualifications in vascular surgery. He publishes and speaks extensively on heart disease. He lives in Pelham Manor, New York, with his wife and three children.

GREGORY FRICCHIONE, M.D., is currently an associate professor of psychiatry at Harvard Medical School and associate chief of psychiatry at Massachusetts General Hospital, where he is director of the Division of Psychiatry and Medicine and the Division of International Psychiatry. Previously, he served as director of the Mental Health Task Force at the Carter Center in Atlanta, Georgia, where he worked with Rosalynn Carter and former president Jimmy Carter on public and international mental health issues and policy. Dr. Fricchione received his M.D. from New York University School of Medicine and is board certified in psychiatry with additional qualifications in geriatric psychiatry and psychosomatic medicine. Dr. Fricchione has been an active researcher, making contributions to the treatment of patients with catatonia and management of cardiac patients who suffer from comorbid psychiatric conditions. He is a coauthor of the *MGH Handbook on General Hospital Psychiatry* (2004) and *Catatonia: From Psychopathology to Neurobiology* (2004).